The RECOVERING SORORITY GIRLS' GUIDE To a Year's Worth of PERFECT PARTIES

Kristina "Morgan" Rose
and Deandra "Brooksie" Brooks

Andrews McMeel
Publishing
Kansas City

To our families, especially our parents
Jim and Alice Morgan and Dave and Linda Brooks,
and friends for their constant, absolute support
and for showing us all the reasons we have to celebrate.
And most important,
for Recovering Sorority Girls everywhere!

05 06 07 08 09 TNS 10 9 8 7 6 5 4 3 2 1

ISBN: 0-7407-5040-2

Library of Congress Control Number: 2004111535

Illustrations by Sean Simon Ramirez
Book design by Holly Camerlinck

Attention: Schools and Businesses

Andrews McMeel books are available at quantity discounts with bulk purchase for educational, business, or sales promotional use. For information, please write to: Special Sales Department, Andrews McMeel Publishing, 4520 Main Street, Kansas City, Missouri 64111.

ACKNOWLEDGMENTS

Morgan and Brooksie would like to thank the world's most visionary literary agent Linda Konner, and everyone at Andrews McMeel, for their RSG joie de vivre and for guiding us through the publishing process.

Our "beta" readers, Carie Ketz, Kristen Baldwin, Ginna DuRard, and Heather Callahan Stevens, who read the good, the bad, the ugly, and the first draft.

A special "thank you" to Carie for taking the leap of faith and test driving our recipes at her own parties. Thank you for accepting your bid; your tiara is in the mail.

And also we have to thank Jim Johnston. Jim honestly believed in us before we ever believed in ourselves and always made time to read our latest draft. Without you, we never would have gotten this far. You're the best unpublished author in America, and a great friend. It's just too bad that you can't be a *sister*.

Finally, Morgan and Brooksie have to thank Joe and Marshall. Their love and support have made it a lot easier to party.

CONTENTS

THE SOCIETY OF
RECOVERING SORORITY GIRLS

CHAPTER BYLAWS AND RUSH GUIDELINES

The Society of Recovering Sorority Girls is an elite organization devoted to living a life less ordinary.

ARTICLE I.
FOUNDING STATEMENT

Our mission is to educate people everywhere in fabulous party-hosting techniques. It all comes back to one simple premise—everything we need to know about throwing great parties, we learned in our collegiate sorority.

Sometimes, Greek life can get a bad rap. But we've found that it truly teaches many valuable lessons, both serious and frivolous. Where else can you learn how to make really great tissue paper flowers for a homecoming float, the difference between formal versus semiformal dress, and, even more important, the fine distinction between casual versus dressy-casual?

After graduation, however, you are no longer a sorority girl. At that point, Greek or independent, you have entered collegiate recovery and are eligible to *rush*[1] Rho Sigma Gamma, the Society of Recovering Sorority Girls, or RSG. An RSG needs to find an adult outlet for fun. Those wild nights with the entire water polo team as your party "dates" and midweek beach road trips with your *pledge sisters* are behind you. At twenty-three, thirty-three, and forty-three such things are just unseemly, not to mention no longer practical. After all, it's not easy to meet an entire water polo team once you've left the dorm behind.

The time, therefore, has arrived for you to seize your destiny and to develop the skills required to throw parties that will take you into this new stage of life with the style and elegance that an RSG member deserves.

In the end, there's nothing better than a well-planned party. Our role as the founders of the Society of Recovering Sorority Girls indicates the adoption of a wholesale entertaining lifestyle. We have, therefore, transformed our lives into one nonstop party. All our party pursuits have taught us that not everyone has developed that sorority girl instinct to please her guests. It is the goal of our organization to spread this wisdom.

ARTICLE II.
MEMBERSHIP

So how do you know if RSG is for you? A girl is ready to *rush* the Society of Recovering Sorority Girls when she has reached the point where she would like the option of a chair and prefers not to be ankle-deep in beer cans at the end of the night. And let's be honest—now you have even more reasons to party than you ever did in college. The boring details of work, bills, and all the other yucky stuff that make up everyday life require escape.

As many of you already know, the central point in *collegiate* sorority life is membership recruitment—aka *rush*. During sorority *rush*, *chapters* are called upon to host up to fifteen separate, well-articulated parties in one week. Parties must be entertaining and accessible to the university's entire *rush group*. Under these conditions, we, your faithful founders, learned how to match decoration colors, properly present menus, and make lots of high-quality party chatter.

No sorority can survive without generating new members. The *rush* process of the Society of Recovering Sorority Girls calls upon you, *rushee*, to entice new members of your

---

1. If you are going to party with the Recovering Sorority Girls, you'll need to learn to speak the language. Check out the Glossary of Sorority Speak Terms for the translations of the italicized words throughout the text.

urban/suburban friendship tribe with a series of well-thrown parties. In this quest for like-minded partyers you must cast a wide net and get to know a variety of people. Our *collegiate* experiences taught us that your new best friend may not reveal herself through a first impression and she definitely will not reveal herself if you have invited her into an awkward and user-unfriendly social situation. As a result, you must identify comfort zones and dedicate yourself to providing a social milieu that exists within those zones.

ARTICLE III.
SERVICE

The Society of Recovering Sorority Girls is committed to public service. When properly hosted, a party is a public service—it gives your guests something to look forward to and creates excitement within your social circle. When a party falls flat, it's just a waste of time in everyone's busy lives. A party that fails to articulate our principles of creating guest comfort zones is likely a bad party, and bad parties generate resentment, making people reluctant to partake of your hospitality in the future. The adult equivalent of being cut from *rush*!

So to facilitate your service activities, we'll give you important how-to guides covering crucial party topics such as:

- Appropriately articulating your party theme.
- Making a little money look like extravagance.
- Selecting your menu and beverages without breaking the bank or sacrificing the theme.
- Devising simple, user-friendly menus that won't drain your time, make you a prisoner to your kitchen, or expand your waistline.
- Making the best use of technology without people wondering if you work for Microsoft.
- Mixing different sets of friends with grace.
- Establishing your reputation as a party goddess and generally saving your social life.

In addition to spreading the party wisdom of the Society of Recovering Sorority Girls, we have provided a year's worth of sensational social events. Unless otherwise specified, every event anticipates a guest list of twenty and includes a theme, a complete menu, decorations, mood points, and, above all, the attitude and vision you need to pull it off. You'll also notice we're about simplicity, and be surprised by how a little attention to detail can take an ordinary object from great to first rate. We haven't forgotten that parties, like life, should be fun—and so is this book. We've included some top-ten lists, helpful quizzes, and loads of insight—aka rants—to help you transition from a *rushee* into a *pledge* of the Society of Recovering Sorority Girls.

ARTICLE IV.
SISTERHOOD

If throwing a party by yourself seems too overwhelming, take a page from our book—pun intended—and grab a friend whose judgment you trust to act as your *rush* partner. RSG's faithful founders don't go it alone; why on earth would you? So find your suitable *rush* partner and the two of you can divide the work and cost, while you multiply the fun, guest list, and creativity.

Good luck, and welcome to *rush*. We look forward to your contributions to Rho Sigma Gamma.

JANUARY

NEW MARTINI'S EVE

*Resolve to shake yourself into a New Year. Besides,
Dick Clark is so much funnier after you've had three martinis!*

CONCEPT

Sick of overpriced, flat hotel parties with bad food, crowded bars, and bald guys named Stu looking down your dress while asking if you have anyone to kiss at midnight? Host a martini-tasting party. This sophisticated home-entertaining concept will leave your guests admiring your creativity and casual elegance. One word of warning: Do *not* drink the entire recipe before moving on to the next martini. Confine yourself to one round of 3-ounce tasting portions of each recipe per guest and *then* revisit the yummiest entrants. In our experience the yummiest include the Red Velvet Swing, Crazy in da Coconut, and of course, the venerable appletini.

You, as the hostess, will graciously provide the gin and vodka. Your guests will bring their favorite martini recipes and the other ingredients needed to shake till you drop. People sample as many martini recipes as they like, and all guests participate in the evening's other bonding activity, the Resolution Board. Throw in a sexy lighting scheme and some lounge music and your guests will be shakin' in the New Year in style.

The martini-tasting idea provides you with two critical advantages:

1. It allows you, the hostess, to provide a stocked bar without breaking the budget; and

2. It creates great preparty buzz as your guests compete among themselves for the night's favorite recipe.

DECORATIONS

1 keg of gold curling ribbon

30 martini glasses

At least two gold charger plates

30 white or metallic-colored paper or plastic plates

40 white or metallic-colored cocktail napkins

30 sets of plastic cutlery

1 22 x 28 inches piece of white or white with gold accents poster board

1 black fine-point Magic Marker or gold-paint pen

400 white Christmas tree lights per every 1,500 square feet of party space and tape or thumbtacks to attach them

1 roll (15 square feet) of plain metallic wrapping paper

1 package of 50 white tea lights in aluminum cups per every 1,500 square feet of party space

Tie the curling ribbon around the stems of your cocktail glasses. We recommend gold, but silver or sparkling will also do. Then place the cocktail glasses on the gold chargers so that once your guests arrive, the stemware will be attractively presented.

Scatter small pieces of curling ribbon among the chargers and food table, through the chandelier (if there is one), or any open spaces that you think need some sparkle. Think of it as easy-to-clean up confetti.

A plain piece of white poster board becomes your Resolution Board—this party's *bump* or conversation transitioner. Write the number of the New Year across the board and hang it in a prominent area. As guests arrive, give them a Magic Marker to write their New Year's resolutions on the board and then sign their names. They can read what other guests have written, and you, as the hostess, can use these facts to *bump* people into conversation and *bump* yourself back out into *rotation*. For example, "Bob, this is my coworker, Jane. Her resolution is very similar to yours. She wants to go to the gym three times a week to get in better shape. Why don't you tell her how you found your personal trainer?"

Create a lighting atmosphere. String your white Christmas tree lights decoratively around windows, doors, and other surfaces that can be easily defined and framed by the lights, e.g., balcony railing, fireplace, bar, etc. Brooksie likes to use thumbtacks to attach the lights to the walls of the room, just below the ceiling.

Metallic wrapping paper + tea lights = very shiny light! Cut squares or interesting shapes out of the metallic wrapping paper to place under elegant groupings of tea lights and other candles you may already own. Focus on the different levels of your room—higher bookshelves, the coffee table, mantel—and don't forget the bathroom.

With the lights turned low and the shimmer of the ribbon and paper, your party space should glimmer and shine like your grandma's polished silver. You can transform your party space from an everyday living room to an elegantly decorated martini lounge in about an hour. Further, your decorations have enhanced your cocktail party theme through their upscale simplicity. Not to mention that everyone looks better in a softer light, and it cuts down the time it takes to put on those beer, or in this case, martini-goggles. By midnight, your best friend's coworker, Art, will have transformed from a simple accountant into a knight in shining armor.

Designate an area that will be the serving area for the food; typically a table, a buffet, or pass-through bar will work well. Arrange the plates, napkins, and cutlery on or adjacent to the designated food station. Be mindful of creating positive traffic flow. Remember that whenever you see a listing of plates, napkins, and cutlery in a party's decorations list, those items should be placed with the party's food offerings in a way to maximize efficient movement of guests through the "buffet area."

 ## FOOD

For the food, we recommend an Italian-themed menu. Not only is it super easy and cheap, it makes a traditional and comforting kind of menu that most people enjoy. Plus the bread and pasta will prepare even sensitive tummies for the martini onslaught. (Remember, *rushees*,

MENU

Antipasto Tray with Crusty Bread, Mozzarella, Salami, and Olives
Pasta Bar with Easy Homemade Red (Marinara) Sauce and Pesto Sauce
Cannoli

For up to 20 guests

eight martinis is not called dinner, no matter how tasty they are.)

Antipasto Tray

2 large crusty baguettes
1 pound assorted salami, sliced
1 pound mozzarella, sliced
Two 16-ounce cans whole black olives, drained

Arrange the baguettes, cut into slices, and the salami and mozzarella slices on your nice serving pieces, along with the olives. Preferably use crystal or gold to accent the decorations.

PASTA BAR

Although the pesto can easily be prepackaged or from a mix, it is much less popular to do so for the red (marinara) sauce. Many people, especially those from the much-ballyhooed Long Island area, have a severe aversion to "jar sauce." So, Morgan's Italian-American husband taught her this easy approach to red sauce using the ingredients below, which he assures us will pacify most tastes.

Red (Marinara) Sauce

2 tablespoons olive oil
2 tablespoons chopped garlic (fresh or from a jar)
1 tablespoon chopped dried basil
2 tablespoons dried oregano

Crushed red pepper to taste
One 16-ounce can tomato sauce
Two 28-ounce cans of tomato puree
Pinch of baking soda
1 teaspoon black pepper

It all starts with 1 tablespoon of olive oil in a nonstick small skillet or other suitable fry pan. Place on medium heat and add the chopped garlic, basil, oregano, and crushed red pepper. Sauté until the garlic is slightly browned, about 3 to 5 minutes.

In a large saucepot combine the tomato sauce, tomato puree, remaining tablespoon of olive oil, and the pinch of baking soda. The baking soda will cause the acid in the tomatoes to bubble. Stir until the bubbling subsides.

Add the sautéed mixture and the black pepper to the saucepot. Stir and heat over low to medium heat until the sauce is bubbling again and then reduce the heat to the low or warm setting. Allow the sauce to simmer lightly for at least 1 hour, stirring occasionally.

That was actual home cooking and it wasn't hard at all!

Pesto Sauce

Four 6.3-ounce jars ready-made
      pesto sauce

Since you purchased the pesto sauce in a jar, some other fool has already done the cooking. All you need to do is heat it according to the directions on the side of the jar. Serve it in a pretty bowl. When someone asks if you made the sauce, say yes. Don't feel compelled to get into the specifics on the pesto, though.

Pasta and Extras

Three 16-ounce boxes penne pasta

20 mini cannoli (filled or shells sold with filling)

One (1¼ pound) package freshly grated Parmesan cheese

Fix the penne and premade cannoli according to package directions. Provide Parmesan cheese for sprinkling atop the dishes.

Martinis

Five 750-ml bottles vodka

One 750-ml bottle gin

One 750-ml bottle vermouth

These are the basics for any good martini. Different people like them fixed different ways, so count on your guests to provide their own recipes.

MAKE THE MOOD COME ALIVE

A proper cocktail party like this requires cocktail music. We suggest Frank Sinatra, Dean Martin, the sound track to *Casino*, etc. Even if your personal selection of Rat Pack recordings is lacking, the public library will let you borrow CDs. While their selections may seem sparse compared to most music stores, borrowing, unlike purchasing, frees up more party budget for important things, like vodka. Of course, around 11:30 P.M. you have to turn on *Dick Clark's New Year's Rockin' Eve*.

You will need one very large bowl for the pasta and two smaller bowls for the sauces. Your faithful founders typically carry forward the gold of the party theme by placing the cooked pasta, which has been tossed lightly with olive oil to prevent sticking, in a clear glass bowl with a gold rim. Serving utensils are placed in the pasta and sauces. Put each of the sauces in one of two smaller gold-rimmed glass bowls. If your serving table is round, the sauce bowls are placed in a cluster surrounding the pasta bowl. If your serving table is square or rectangular, place the bowls in a straight line, starting with the plates and utensils, then the pasta, then the sauces in the smaller gold-rimmed glass bowls in whatever order you choose. When designing your food table, think flow. Analyze your serving area and come up with an arrangement that will allow guests to serve themselves and then move back into *rotation*.

Although your party colors are all things meant to shine, we'll leave the color of table linens and serving plate selection up to you. Here is where traditional party mavens will tell you that the age-old question "paper or plastic?" is the kiss of death, no matter how you answer it. But the Recovering Sorority Girls believe your guests have come to party with you, not watch you pick up scattered dishes and load the dishwasher all night. Moreover, if you know that you will personally sample all fifteen rounds of martinis, we suggest that you select the most dignified disposable plates you can find. After the tenth martini, holding a breakable martini glass is challenge enough. Why complicate matters with a nonpaper plate?

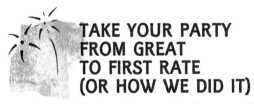

TAKE YOUR PARTY FROM GREAT TO FIRST RATE (OR HOW WE DID IT)

Morgan hand-painted personalized coasters for each guest at the paint-your-own pottery place.

In addition to making impressive party favors, the coasters made it easy to figure out which drink belonged to whom, eliminating embarrassing mixups and wasted liquor.

We also had our guests wear pajamas to keep the party down to earth and encouraged them to stay the night and party into the wee hours of the morning (and early afternoon). Sweats and a T-shirt don't count! They just make you look frumpy. A nice pair of trendy, fifties-style pajamas demonstrates that you understand the theme.

Make arrangements for brunch the next day. If you're adventurous, you and your pajama-clad guests can take the party on the road to the local diner. But if you're feeling timid, we suggest you pick up an array of bagels, juices, and fruits to set out on New Year's Day.

TIMELINE

People need to decide early how they are spending New Year's, so give your guests a little more notice than usual. We suggest telling people, by word of mouth, right before Thanksgiving, because that's when all those bad hotel parties—aka "the competition"—start selling tickets.

Ideally, you would announce your party about one week before Thanksgiving using teaser e-mails. Just a simple line or two to your *rush group* with a subject line of "What will you be shaking at midnight on December 31?" Keep the body simple. Just two or three lines to the effect of "Why, a martini, of course!" "New Martini's Eve is coming, details to follow."

After word of mouth has taken root, it's time for the formal invitations. Your faithful founders are devotees of the online or electronic invitation. Electronic invitations are free and allow you to send out a written invitation while avoiding the hassle of the post office. In addition, electronic invitations also allow prospective guests to see who else is invited and is a great source of preparty buzz.

If your friends are not "e-mail people," then attractive handwritten save-the-date cards or invitations can be substituted wherever your faithful founders direct the use of electronic invitations.

Send your actual e-mail around the first of December, but no later than December 10. Realizing that people have shopping, holiday travel, and other things still going on, don't get upset if they aren't as obsessed as you are with your fabulous upcoming party. They'll be appropriately focused the moment that last Christmas present is unwrapped.

But you, our *rushee* in training, have a holiday schedule too, and that why we say KISS— and we don't mean that thing you do at midnight—Keep It Simple, *Sister*. Simple food, simple decorations, simple clothing, and a simple trip to the liquor store the day of the party. Most liquor outlets run holiday specials. Going the day of, you'll find it surprisingly not crowded, with only the champagne picked over and good deals on other spirits. According to the liquor store proprietors we talked to, Christmas Eve is the actual date of the rush. It seems that the majority of Americans won't go forward into family gatherings unless appropriately fortified.

After Christmas, in addition to being the optimal liquor-shopping window, is also the best time to make many other party-related purchases because, as all devoted sorority girls know, lots of stuff goes on sale after the holiday! To stretch your money, brave the malls and hit the card stores for curling ribbon, white Christmas tree lights, high-quality paper plates and napkins, a roll of metallic wrapping paper, and white tea lights.

December 30, the day before the party— Tidy up and put away any breakables that could become party casualties. Also, if you haven't already figured out your outfit, do it now!

The night before the party—Undertake your skin care regimen. Pictures will be taken and there is no substitute for the healthy glow of properly maintained skin! Exfoliate! Exfoliate! Exfoliate! But, never exfoliate the day of the party; you'll just be all red and blotchy.

The morning or afternoon of the party—
Make your run to the grocery store and liquor store. Then, go home and make and place your decorations (this should take no more than an hour, depending upon the amount of space that you are working with), allowing enough time to get in the all-important preparty nap and the necessary preparty beauty regimen. Fresh nail polish is a must!

7 P.M.	Begin making the red sauce.
8 P.M.	Boil water for the pasta. Assemble the antipasto plate. If the cannoli were not purchased from the bakery filled, begin spooning bakery filling into shells. Refrigerate them after filling.
8:30 P.M.	Dump the pasta into water.
8:45 P.M.	Put out the antipasto and glassware trays.
9 P.M.	Heat the pesto sauce. Greet guests as they arrive.
9:05 P.M.	Place pasta and sauces on the serving table.
9:10 P.M.	Distribute the first round of martinis to taste (we suggest starting with the Red Velvet Swing).
9:40 P.M.	Repeat above steps as needed.
10:30 P.M.	Put out cannoli.
Midnight	Kiss your date or the one you have a crush on—Happy New Year's!

A WORD ABOUT . . . BUYING LIQUOR

Your faithful founders have consulted with a variety of entertainment publications and what our exhaustive research has taught us is that conventional wisdom dictates the following:

1. A standard-size bottle (of liquor, that is to say, 750 milliliters up to 1 liter) is estimated to yield between eight and twelve servings.
2. The average[1] party guest will consume three drinks.

These standards are simply estimates; it's important to know your guests. If your friends like their drinks strong, then assume only eight servings per bottle. If your friends are not fond of the taste of hard liquor, your average drink-to-guest ratio may be closer to one or two. Our

---

1. Most Recovering Sorority Girls we know tend to consume just slightly above the "average," especially when wearing pajamas.

advice is to calculate what you reasonably think will reflect your guests' tastes and habits and then buy an extra bottle or two. Leftovers can be saved for subsequent parties, and the memory of overabundance is oh so much better than being remembered as the girl who threw the New Year's Eve party where they ran out of hooch!

Also, to make your shopping even easier, get your guests to commit to a recipe when they RSVP. That way, you can decide how much gin and how much vodka you will need. In our case, our guests all selected vodka martini recipes, so no gin was necessary.

CABIN FEVER
BEACH
PARTY

Just because you don't live in the tropies

doesn't mean you don't deserve all the fun of a swim-up bar!

CONCEPT

Just say no to seasonal affective disorder. What better way to forget it's cold and yucky outside than donning a Hawaiian shirt or grass skirt in your own tropical paradise? This party is designed to help you forget it's still the dead of winter. Think tropical!

January isn't our favorite month. Although you have New Year's at the beginning of the month and football playoffs throughout, there's not a whole lot of excitement. Plus unless you live in Florida or Southern California, the weather

sucks. Is there really anything worse than trudging to work in slushy rush hour conditions while it's still dark out only to travel home when it is already dark in more slushy rush hour conditions? Nothing that we have faced, that's for sure.

Clearly, you can't spend the entire month at a tropical all-inclusive resort. You could, but your boss would start to get tweaked and your boyfriend would likely get worried. Survival in style, therefore, calls for the following: lots of light and lots of drinks with little umbrellas. Our Cabin Fever Beach Party gives you both in the comfort of your own living room!

DECORATIONS

Beach towels—all the ones you own, you may even want to borrow a few

1 large Mexican blanket or old sheet

A piece of string long enough to fit between two walls

2 thumbtacks

20 sheets of brightly colored construction paper, 1 sheet per guest; a variety pack from the local craft should cover it

One roll of Scotch tape

20 plastic clothespins

One bottle of sunscreen, 8 oz Hawaiian Tropic Deep Tanning Lotion, SPF 4 smells nice

3 to 5 inflatable beach balls

That ubiquitous box or glass of shells you have from your last trip to the beach

20 flower leis; plastic or silk is fine, 1 per guest, given on arrival

1 Magic Marker

A selection of "fabulous" prizes

30 paper or plastic plates—select a bright color that matches your beach towels

40 paper napkins—select a bright color that matches your beach towels

30 sets of plastic cutlery

40 plastic cups—select a bright color that matches your beach towels

You are bringing a Caribbean all-inclusive resort into your home, so start your decorations with the items you would pack for such a vacation. We suggest covering your sofas and chairs with beach towels. In addition to incorporating your theme, they can also conveniently catch spills—this becomes important when we get to those beach balls. Create additional seating space on the floor by spreading your Mexican blanket or old sheet in the middle of your main party room. This will encourage guests to "lay out."

The electronic invitation will require each guest to bring his or her favorite vacation photo. Using your guests' pictures of the tropics you will create an "ocean-view window" in your "resort." This picture wall is both a great decoration and your conversation *bump*. Before the party, you will hang your string, attached to the wall with the two thumbtacks, one on each end, across one wall within the flow of party traffic, but in a space not impeding party flow. For example, do not put the string near or behind your food table. Instead, hang the string just slightly above eye level across the wall to your bathroom or opposite your TV. You will use your construction paper to make a "frame" for the photo. Go ahead, using your Magic Marker, and label one sheet of construction paper per guest. As the guests arrive, ask them to write the location of where their photo was taken on the construction paper and then place a loop of Scotch tape on the back of the photo, attaching it to the sheet of brightly colored construction paper. Use a clothespin to attach each sheet of construction paper to the string, creating your appropriately hung "framed photo." Once you've assembled all of your guests' photos in this manner, you will most likely have a photo essay of the world's hottest vacation spots, or if your friends are lame, several pictures of Branson, Missouri, Niagara Falls, and Pierre, South Dakota. Our apologies to the residents of these fine cities, but admit it, you vacation somewhere else, too.

And since we've explained how the string and clothespin work, now you're wondering, "What's up with sunscreen in January?" The answer is simple. Your faithful founders believe that (1) there is never a wrong time for sunscreen—protected skin is youthful skin; and (2) parties are an occasion for individuals to meet new and interesting people of similar social circles. Therefore, RSG parties provide several features designed to spark conversation, flirting, and maybe even a little huggy-bear/kissy-face.[2] So put that sunscreen on the coffee table, on the food table, or by the bar. And when you see Jim from marketing, don't be afraid to ask him if he can do your back. He might reach some spots you didn't know you had.

Now let's talk about those inflatable beach balls. Just blow them up and scatter them around. Someone, probably your socially awkward cousin Keith, will spend most of the night playing with one in a corner instead of talking to any girls. Well, except for the girl he apologizes to after knocking her drink over with the ball. But in addition to giving cousin Keith a reason to talk to a girl, the beach balls are the attention to detail that cause your friends to realize you are *rushing* Rho Sigma Gamma!

---

2. The term "huggy-bear/kissy-face" does not include any actions that will warrant an R movie rating. "Huggy-bear/kissy-face" is very PG, or PG-13 tops.

FOOD

The food table should appeal to all five senses. Start by covering the table with a beach towel or colorful sheet. While all of your offerings will tantalize your guests' taste buds, the aroma of the complex chicken marinade should make their mouths water. The colors of the Fruit Kabobs will appeal visually. The crunchy toasted coconut of the macaroons evokes a traditional tropical texture. But what about sound? For sound, nothing beats the roar of the ocean. While the sea won't fit on your food table, the sound of the sea can often be found in seashells. Use that ubiquitous box of seaglass or shells *we know you have* to add a touch of fun to the food table. Just scatter them around the table among the dishes and your guests will notice.

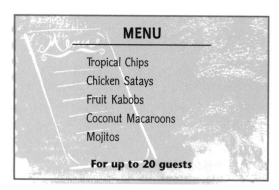

MENU

Tropical Chips

Chicken Satays

Fruit Kabobs

Coconut Macaroons

Mojitos

For up to 20 guests

3. If you were wondering what a satay is, it's chicken on a stick.

Tropical Chips

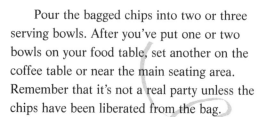

One 7.5-ounce bag yucca chips
    (see Note below)

One 7.5-ounce bag cassava chips
    (see Note below)

Pour the bagged chips into two or three serving bowls. After you've put one or two bowls on your food table, set another on the coffee table or near the main seating area. Remember that it's not a real party unless the chips have been liberated from the bag.

Note: If cassava and yucca chips are not available in your local grocery store or Latino market, substitute any root vegetable chips from the health food section of your major grocer as they contain yucca and several other beet vegetables.

Chicken Satays

The Society of Recovering Sorority Girls firmly believes there is no party menu problem that cannot be solved by putting chicken on sticks. For that reason, we start you early with our sure-fire tropical Chicken Satays.[3]

5 pounds boneless, skinless chicken breasts
Two 12-ounce bottles commercial jerk or
    mojo marinade (check label for
    amount needed relative to chicken)
100 bamboo or wood skewers

Take the chicken breasts and slice them lengthwise into three-inch strips of approximately one-quarter inch in width or 1 ounce in weight. Thread each chicken strip onto the stick, aka skewer. Place the sticks in a deep dish and coat the meat with either the jerk or mojo marinade. To achieve that tropical taste, the chicken should be marinated for 2 hours prior to cooking. If you are bucking for the outstanding *pledge* award, grill the Chicken Satays on your barbecue until the meat is no longer pink, typically about 20 minutes over hot coals. If you are using bamboo skewers, remember to soak the skewers in water for about 30 minutes before threading the chicken on them and putting the skewers on the grill, as the direct flame may burn the wood.

If that simply isn't possible, place the satays on the aluminum-foil[4]-coated cookie sheet or baking pan. Bake in a preheated 350 degree conventional oven for 20 minutes.

We believe that indoor grilling is not time-efficient for a project of this magnitude. Plus the smoke could make your eyes red.

Fruit Kabobs

Now that you've learned how to thread chicken on a stick, it's time to try stacking fruit on a stick. The Fruit Kabobs lend a colorful, tasty, and weight-maintenance-sensitive item to your menu. Not only are they your "vegetable," the colors are so bright they're practically decorations.

Three 24.5-ounce jars of tropical fruit salad
    pineapple and papaya chunks
One 28-ounce jar maraschino cherries
Two 15-ounce cans mandarin oranges
Bamboo or wood skewers

Just open all the cans and jars, drain, and start assembling. On a six-inch wood or bamboo skewer, each kabob should have no more than four pieces of fruit. But that's the only rule; go ahead and get creative.

Macaroons

Two 13-ounce packages coconut macaroons,
    from a box or the bakery—you choose

---

4. The aluminum foil is critical in order to prevent excessive cleaning. Remember, excessive cleaning by *rushees* or *pledges* is a form of hazing and the Society of Recovering Sorority Girls supports the larger Panhellenic resolution against hazing of any kind.

The macaroons come in a box. We don't care if it's a box from the bakery or a box off the shelf of the cookie aisle. You are instructed to remove the macaroons from said box and transfer them to a lovely decorative serving plate or tray. Then you must hide said box in a place your guests will never find it.

Mojitos

Important matters. The signature cocktail. Your faithful founders believe in the power of the signature cocktail. The signature cocktail carries forward the theme of your party, but also contains the essence needed to enliven your guests. Translation: Booze makes people funny. For your visit to the tropics, you *must* serve the current darling of the East Coast bar and coincidentally the national drink of Cuba, the humble mojito. If you haven't run across one at happy hour yet, a mojito is an intoxicating combination of rum, soda, mint leaves, and a hint of lime that transports you to the swinging pre-Fidel Havana. It has to be pre-Fidel because everyone knows Communists don't make good cocktails. It's why they lost the cold war. The mojito is a delicate elixir, requiring intermediate-level bartending skills. If you've ever watched a pro make one, you'll note the use of a simple syrup shaken with light white

rum and ten fresh mint leaves. This base is poured into a highball glass, topped with seltzer water and half a lime, cut in wedges. While this method is authentic, it may ruin your party mojo, so we have "cheated" the recipe to get you back to your guests with your yummy Latin treats, *tout de suite.*

Six 12-ounce containers frozen limeade
    concentrate
3 liters light white rum
Six .66-ounce packages fresh mint
4 liters cold seltzer water
5 fresh limes, cut into wedges
50 drink umbrellas

Using a blender, combine one 12-ounce container of frozen limeade concentrate and 2 cups of rum. Blend thoroughly. Because the limeade is sweetened, you are getting your simple syrup along with the lime flavor. Pour the limeade-rum mix into a punch bowl. Next, destem one package of mint, so that you are working just with the actual leaves. Add the package of fresh, destemmed mint leaves to the limeade-rum mix. Using a wooden spoon, aggressively stir the mint leaves into the liquid. Although you don't want to break the mint leaves, you do want to pound a little flavor out of them. Add 20 ounces of cold seltzer and stir.

Add the lime wedges. Serve over ice, and garnish with the drink umbrellas. (This should make approximately ten drinks.) Repeat as needed, singing ". . . at the Copa, Copacabana, the hottest club north of Havana" to the rhythm of the blender.

MAKE THE MOOD COME ALIVE

For music, nothing says resort like Jimmy Buffett or Bob Marley. We especially like Jimmy Buffett's *Don't Stop the Carnival* and Bob Marley's *Legend.* If you decide to employ some Jimmy Buffett, remember to think outside the box. "Margaritaville" is fun but overplayed and "Why Don't We Get Drunk and Screw" can be icky if you are locked in conversation with an undesirable coworker when it comes on the stereo. Feel free to add some Beach Boys or California punk-pop and ska favorites like Sublime, Blink-182, and Reel Big Fish for depth.

But you can't forget the classics. We're talking Frankie and Annette in *Beach Blanket Bingo.* And if you can figure out exactly how to play beach blanket bingo, we strongly encourage you to do so.

For a truly enjoyable party, your faithful founders believe that an ice breaker activity is required. This activity serves as an automatic *bump* and *rotation,* plus it feeds the competitive needs of certain guests. Come on, admit it, you know who they are.

The dress code for this party is resort wear. As such, this party cries out for a hard-core, ugly Hawaiian shirt contest. Within the last ten years, ugly Hawaiian shirts have become available in stores such as Neiman Marcus and Target. So since you know your guests probably have them, they should bring them out for judging, admiration, and ridicule from their friends and associates. As hostess, you or your designee can narrate this "catwalk" and let the guests determine which competitor will receive the fabulous prizes you've provided. Popular vote rules, unless you are single. Then the cutest guy, or the guy you have a crush on, wins.

Now, let's talk furniture configuration. Your party space should reflect the vast expanse of the beach and ocean. In addition to incorporating your theme, this will also maximize the party flow. So shove what you've got up against the walls.

While your faithful founders are usually strong advocates for the softer lighting created by candles and decorative lights, we must abandon that belief in times of trauma, like winter. Your sun-deprived body needs light, so turn them on! All of them! If you have a friend who is an admitted depressive and is in possession of a light box, *take it*. Just make sure you invite that person (and the light box) to this party to prevent further trauma, though. Should someone dare complain about the excessive light, just explain that the tropical sun requires protective gear and offer a pair of plastic sunglasses; make a mental note that this guest just doesn't get a properly executed theme. Consider social exile.

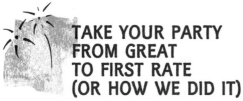

TAKE YOUR PARTY FROM GREAT TO FIRST RATE (OR HOW WE DID IT)

No trip to the beach is complete without that oh-so-lovely feeling of sand between your toes. So invest in a cheap kiddie pool and some sand. Put a brightly colored plastic tablecloth down on the kitchen floor, then the kiddie pool and add sand. Feel free to hide a few "buried treasures" for your guests to find.

Intensify the experience of aroma by adding a few ocean-scented candles. Also add a small arrangement of tropical flowers in each bathroom.

Erect a volleyball net, low to the ground, in your party space. Guests can use the inflatable beach balls to play on their knees.

Check with a local travel agent to see if they have cheap posters of tropical destinations. Hang them on both sides of your bathroom doors.

If you or any of your friends have a surfboard, by all means, incorporate it into your party as a decoration.

TIMELINE

When planning this party, be sure you don't conflict with football play-off games. We recommend holding your gathering on a Friday night or perhaps on the Saturday during the break between the play-offs and the Super Bowl. Consult the football schedule, and set the date.

The theme is counterintuitive to the season, so you may need to send out a few teaser e-mails to get your stodgier guests in the mood. If this is the case, you've got no time to lose and must start 3 days after New Year's.

Two weeks before the party—Send the electronic invitation. Be sure to advise your guests of the resort wear dress code, Hawaiian shirts encouraged. Select your faux tan regimen—booth or spray-on!

One week before the party—Buy any decorations you do not currently own.

Two days before the party—Exfoliate, moisturize, and tidy your party space.

The morning of the party—Go to the grocery store and the liquor store.

4:20 P.M.	Cut and skewer the chicken, place in the marinade, and refrigerate.
5:30 P.M.	Decorate the party space.
6 P.M.	Prepare the Fruit Kabobs; refrigerate.
6:20 P.M.	Remove the Chicken Satay from the refrigerator and cook.
6:25 P.M.	Finish your look, put on that grass skirt or sarong and cap it off with a bikini top. You're tan; your guests should be given the opportunity to bask in your glow.
6:40 P.M.	Remove satays from oven and place on several platters.
6:45 P.M.	Prepare the first batch of mojitos; set out the Fruit Kabobs and macaroons.
7 P.M.	"Lei" each guest as he or she arrives.
9 P.M.	Start the ugly Hawaiian shirt contest.
9:30 P.M.	Declare an ugly Hawaiian shirt winner, award prizes.

A WORD ABOUT . . . PRIZES

Prizes are a great way to get guests to buy into your ice breaker activity. After all, who can resist the chance to be a winner? Even if all you've won is a can of turtle wax or a box of Rice-A-Roni. Hey, if it was good enough for 1970's game shows, it's good enough for your friends! Besides, you are on a party budget, and no one is really expecting to walk away with a brand-new car—unless it's the Matchbox kind—so get creative.

Recycle that ugly gift your aunt Tillie got you for Christmas, or hit the kiddie prize machines at the grocery store or arcade. The wackier the prize, the longer your guests will be talking about it. To make sure the competition is fierce, it's best to keep the prizes under wraps until the contest is completed. Bottom line, the more random, the better. Who can deny the conversational power of having won a can of cheap, domestic nonalcoholic beer?

RSVP? OR FRENCH DOESN'T HAVE TO BE SCARY!

A RANT BY MORGAN

Why is it that normally considerate guests and treasured friends are so resistant to proper RSVP practice? The only explanation that I can come up with is that people misinterpret the French meaning behind the well-known but apparently inscrutable acronym. O.K., let's demystify, *rushees*.

RSVP is French for *répondez, s'il vous plaît*. A literal, translation is: "Reply, if you please." The intended translation, however, is: "Please reply."

Translations that are definitely incorrect include: "Let me know *only* if you plan to attend" or "Let me know only if you plan *not* to attend." Unfortunately, these two approaches appear to be the most universally applied.

When guests fail to say yes or no, they place their hostess in an unnecessarily elevated state of stress. How much food to buy? How many party favors to procure?

Many guests avoid responding because they think, "Oh, we're such good friends, surely she'll know that I'll be there." If you're really *that* close, be a good friend and let your hostess plan. Still others hide behind the weak excuse that they don't want to hurt their hostess's feelings by saying no to the invitation. As the song says, sometimes you've gotta be cruel to be kind. Look, I'd rather a guest give me a definite no that shows that he or she received and considered the invitation than be forced to plan around a series of nonresponses.

Simply put: If someone thinks enough of you to invite you to a fabulous event, think enough of that person to respond.

If you find that certain of your friends are serial nonresponders who show without an RSVP or fail to respond in total to a series of invitations, may I suggest my personal "three strikes rule": three nonresponses and no more invitations for you for at least a year. You'd be surprised what an effective etiquette tool social exile can be.

Chapter Two

FEBRUARY

CHINESE NEW YEAR'S PARTY

Fortune cookie says a great party is in your future!

CONCEPT

Everyone is at least a little fascinated by Chinese culture. From Bruce Lee to Jackie Chan from chicken chow mein to General Tso's chicken, Chinese culture is cool, well except for the whole human rights record. But if the United Nations can accept the Chinese and ignore this problem, so can you! Plus *every* city in America has a Chinese takeout to provide menu inspiration. How hard could this be?

This party is a celebration of the popular elements of Chinese culture and works well

DECORATIONS

6 Chinese paper lanterns per main party room

3 strings white Christmas tree lights per 1,500 square feet of party space

18 sheets of red construction paper

3 black Magic Markers

1 wand-shaped lighter

Wood glue

1 pair of chopsticks per guest plus 12 pairs
    for scrolls—restaurant-quality with red
    paper wrapping is best
1 roll of Scotch tape
2 kegs of gold curling ribbon (for 20 guests)
2 kegs of red curling ribbon (for 20 guests)
3 bamboo mats to use as trivets for the hot
    dishes on the food table
30 red paper or plastic plates
40 red napkins
Assorted citrus candles
30 sets of plastic cutlery
20 red or white hot beverage cups
20 wineglasses or small plastic glasses

with both small and large invitation lists. But fear not, it does not involve fireworks, so it's clearly family-room friendly.

Hang the paper lanterns from the ceiling, beginning in the corners of the room, working toward the center. Use your white Christmas tree lights to give the lanterns some glow by attaching them to the ceiling, winding them through the lanterns, creating an under-the-stars effect.

Next, make your Chinese astrology scrolls. This requires some research, but fear not, you can get it done by using either a place mat from your favorite Chinese restaurant or by getting the information on the Internet. On a sheet of red construction paper, use your black Magic Marker to write the name of a Chinese Zodiac sign—in Chinese astrology this is an animal—the birth years for that sign, and a few personality characteristics associated with it. Try to find some traits that describe your guests. If you don't have sorority-girl-quality handwriting, type this information on the computer and print it out on the red construction paper. Next, we'll give the scrolls an ancient look by carefully singeing the edges of the paper. Your faithful founders suggest you do this with a candle wand, as it gives you maximum control over your burn pattern and keeps your freshly manicured fingers far from the flame. To complete the scrolls, use the wood glue to attach a single chopstick to the top and bottom of the scroll. Voilà! Instant Chinese tapestries! Hang them with the Scotch tape in your party spaces and be sure to reserve a few for the bathrooms. Don't throw away the extra construction paper. You'll need it later.

On to the curling ribbon. Your faithful founders have never met a chandelier that couldn't be transformed by the magic that is curling ribbon. Use the curling ribbon to add beautiful gold and red touches to wherever it is needed. Think food table, think coffee and end tables, think stemware, think banisters, and don't forget doorknobs. It's a simple little idea, and people may not notice it, but that's because no one immediately picks up on the ambiance that is created by the perfectly decorated party space. But like an upscale restaurant, they will notice if it's lacking. The devil is in the details.

MENU

Chicken and Snow Peas
Veggie Stir-Fry
Jasmine, Brown, or Black Rice
Crispy Noodles with Dipping Sauce
Fresh Orange Segments and Fortune Cookies
Plum Wine or Riesling
Tea Service

For up to 20 guests

Chicken and Snow Peas

5 pounds boneless, skinless chicken breasts

3 teaspoons chopped fresh garlic

3 teaspoons ground ginger

¾ cup fat-free, reduced-sodium
    chicken broth

1½ cups reduced-sodium soy sauce

6 teaspoons cornstarch

Three 5-ounce cans water chestnuts, drained

Two 8-ounce packages frozen snow peas,
    thawed

Crushed red pepper to taste (optional)

Unless your family owns a Chinese restaurant, no single wok will be able to cook all this chicken at once. So, we'll need to do some math here. Slice your chicken breasts into 1/2- to 1/4-inch cubes. Divide your chicken cubes into three roughly equal batches. Spray either a large skillet or wok, preferably a wok, with a fat-free cooking spray, add 1 teaspoon chopped garlic and 1 teaspoon ground ginger. Sauté until the garlic is browned, approximately 5 minutes over medium heat. Add the first batch of chicken cubes, 1/4 cup chicken broth, and 1/2 cup soy sauce. Stirring often, brown the chicken for approximately 10 to 15 minutes, then add 2 teaspoons cornstarch, 5 ounces drained water chestnuts, 6 ounces snow peas, and crushed red pepper. Heat until the sauce thickens and the vegetables are warm. This will take approximately 3 minutes. Transfer to a large, but decorative casserole dish. Place in an oven preheated to warm (250 degrees) to keep this entrée hot until your guests arrive. Sorry, you've only just made a third of the recipe, so you will need to repeat this process two more times or call Martha Stewart and see if you can borrow her industrial kitchen. But don't cry, *rushee*, the entire process should take less than an hour.

Veggie Stir-Fry

Two 16-ounce packages vegetable stir-fry (you pick the brand)

Prepare Veggie Stir-Fry according to the instructions on the back of the bag. Hey, we don't know what brand you picked.

Rice

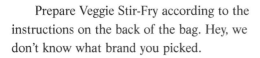

6 cups jasmine, brown, or black rice (your choice)

All rice is not created equal. The time and manner of preparation depends greatly on the type of rice you choose. If you have selected instant rice, you will need to match the amount of rice to the amount of water in the pot, and cook time will take approximately 5 minutes. If, however, taste and not time is your paramount concern, a menu like this cries out for the dressy-casual or dressy rice equivalent. We suggest a nice jasmine rice. If your tastes run to the whole grains or you are more of a culinary adventurer, then use a high-quality brown or black rice. Jasmine, brown, or black rice can be found at most major supermarkets. For example, Mahatma brand is widely available. When in doubt, consult the directions on the package; they won't steer you wrong.

Crispy Noodles and Dipping Sauces

Two 16-ounce packages crispy noodles
One 8-ounce jar sweet and sour sauce
One 8-ounce jar hot mustard sauce

Just dump the crispy noodles into serving bowls. Pour the sweet and sour sauce and the hot mustard into smaller bowls. Place one set of bowls on the food table and another set on the coffee table.

Oranges and Fortune Cookies

Cut five fresh oranges into segments. Alternate the fresh orange pieces and the fortune cookies on decorative plates. You should have approximately twenty fresh orange slices and twenty fortune cookies, at least one for each guest.

Tea Service

Find a lovely tray. Maybe you already own one. Your tray should be preferably Asian or Asian-look, red lacquer or gold. The tray should be large enough to accommodate three saucers and a large teapot for hot water. Each saucer should hold a different type of tea. One for green, one for white, and one for herbal. Just like the rice shouldn't be instant, go that extra mile and find some special teas. In recent years both green and white teas have dramatically increased in popularity in the United States. Green teas undergo the least amount of processing of commercial-grade teas. When brewed, they will be yellow-green in color. Newer in popularity is white tea. White tea is grown in China's Fujian Province and is made only of springtime tea buds, which are picked before they open. If your town doesn't have a high-quality tea merchant, specialty teas are widely available on your party-planning friend the Internet. San Francisco's Ten Ren Tea Company operates a vigorous Web business with decent shipping rates. Visit them at www.tenren.com. There, now you have no excuse for offering your guests an assortment of Lipton and Earl Grey.

Sweet Wine Assortment
Ten 750-ml bottles of plum wine or Riesling

As for your signature cocktail, sweeter wines like plum wine or Rieslings pair well with the spicy flavors of Asian food. While plum wine is more traditional, Rieslings will present a greater variety to your guests. You could offer various wines from Washington, California, Australia, and perhaps a local vineyard's Riesling. Remember to chill appropriately. Open and serve.

MAKE THE MOOD COME ALIVE

Kung-Fu movies have become one of the most westernized facets of Chinese popular culture. And besides, Jet Li is hot and Chow Yun-Fat isn't half bad either. So pick up a few Kung-Fu movies to have playing in the background. *Crouching Tiger, Hidden Dragon* or anything by Jackie Chan will have the appropriate visual appeal. Remember it's not really about entertainment, it's part of your decor.

This party's evening activity draws on ye olde *collegiate* tradition of the *mixer*. At every *mixer*, the *social chair* racks her brain to come up with an activity that requires people while still sober to talk to members of the opposite sex. Popular variations of this time-honored tradition include the "Nuts and Bolts" and the Hawaiian-themed "Lei Me, Tie Me."[1] Our suggestion for this *mixer* in your home is to make Chinese astrology name tags for your guests. Not only do they tie in wonderfully with the decor, they also provide instant introductions and conversation starters. So use the remaining red construction paper to cut out rectangles. If you happen to have scalloped craft scissors, use those to cut the red construction paper rectan-

---

1. For more information about "traditional" mixer types please visit www.recoveringsororitygirls.com.

gles. As they arrive, guests will be led to a table with name tags and Magic Markers. Instruct your guests to write their names and their Chinese astrology signs on their name tags. The total effect should mirror the ubiquitous Chinese restaurant paper place mat.

The lights should be dimmed, as you don't want to overpower the effect of your twinkling stars, aka those white Christmas tree lights, up on your ceiling. Your faithful founders suggest you supplement those stars with several citrus-scented candles. It's still winter and probably cold. The citrus scent will lift moods and honor the sense of smell. Not to mention that acknowledging feng shui by tantalizing all five senses, including the oft-forgotten sense of smell, showcases your RSG party know-how!

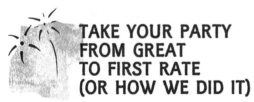

TAKE YOUR PARTY FROM GREAT TO FIRST RATE (OR HOW WE DID IT)

Dress up your food table with a silk tablecloth. No, this is not as overboard as it sounds, but it does involve a trip to the fabric store. Before you go, measure your food table, taking into consideration how far you want the tablecloth to hang over the table. Once you are armed with your measurements, it's time to purchase a piece of Chinese silk fabric and some double-sided fabric tape. Take it home and use the double-sided fabric tape to hide any rough edges.[2]

Spend a little more time in your kitchen the day before your party and make the fortune cookies. Making your own fortune cookies allows you to personalize the fortunes for each guest. But don't worry, we haven't gone crazy. Check around, certain stores and museums sell kits with directions for just this sort of thing. So go buy one and then go wild and type up some truly outrageous fortunes that will cause your guests to double over with laughter. Something like "a hot brunette with legs from here to Memphis is in your future" for that guy some lucky brunette you know has a crush on.

Do a little research into feng shui, an ancient Chinese discipline used as a method to ensure health, wealth, and harmony, and use it to your advantage. While the literal translation means wind and water, it is a study of environment, and in your case, a party environment. For example, since the southwest corner of your home governs love, place an indoor fountain there. Or open your windows for 20 minutes before the party to let fresh *chi* and good fortune into your home.

---

2. While this idea is first rate, we certainly don't expect you to sew! See note 4 on page 15 regarding hazing.

TIMELINE

Chinese New Year falls between late January and late February. It's best to host this party the weekend closest to the actual date. So consult a calendar and select your party date.

Two weeks before the party—Send out your e-mail invitation. Purchase craft supplies and a bulk bag of chopsticks.

The day before the party—Make Chinese astrology scrolls. Cut paper for name tags. Procure movies.

The morning of the party—Purchase ingredients, wine, and paper goods. Chill the plum wine or Riesling. Winter can be hard on the skin. Get a day spa facial to give you that healthy glow.

4 P.M.	String white Christmas tree lights, hang lanterns, and place candles.
4:45 P.M.	Make curling ribbon decorations, hang Chinese astrology scrolls, and set out name tags.
5:15 P.M.	Cut the chicken into cubes.
5:30 P.M.	Set out the pea pods to thaw.
5:45 P.M.	Finish your hair and makeup.
6 P.M.	Start the Chicken and Snow Peas batches.

6:30 P.M.	Start the rice if you are not using instant.
6:45 P.M.	Put the bowls of crunchy noodles and sauces on the food table and coffee table.
6:50 P.M.	Light the candles and arrange the orange segments and fortune cookies on plates. Set up the tea service. Set the food table, using the bamboo mats as trivets.
7 P.M.	Greet guests as they arrive and insist they wear a nametag.
7:10 P.M.	Prepare and serve the Vegetable Stir-Fry. Boil the water for tea.

A WORD ABOUT . . . KNOWING YOUR GUESTS

As a Rho Sigma Gamma *rushee*, one of your most important responsibilities is making your guests feel comfortable. Your faithful founders firmly believe that if your guests do not feel comfortable, they certainly won't have a good time. After all, guests enjoying themselves are the most important party decorations. But in order to create that guest-friendly atmosphere, you need to know a little about your guests.

To demonstrate through example, we thought we'd tell you a little about some of our guests who assisted in the research needed to write this guide. Both Heathers are vegetarians. Marshall prefers red wine to white, but Tanya is allergic to the sulfites in red wine. Ed likes to mix drinks, and while he makes awesome martinis, you can't let him serve any of his creations near an open flame. Lil' Jimmy can be shy, but always enjoys the *mixer* activities. Savvy can need a little coaxing to leave her neighborhood, but once out she always ends up having a good time and could be a stand-up comic if she tried.

So let's break it down. Do any of your guests have food restrictions or special dietary needs that may require menu tweaking? What about beverages? If a large portion of your guest list does not imbibe, be sure to have plenty of alternatives on hand. Personalities count. If you have some friends that mix like oil and water, don't invite both of them to your party. Use your more outgoing invitees to get the games started, and give some of the shyer guests little jobs like making sure there's always music playing.

The more you know about your guests, the better your party will be. Your knowledge will guide you in your selection of traits for the Chinese astrology scrolls and should you choose to make your party first rate, those personalized fortunes (from the fortune cookies) will be hysterical. What you know about those who attend your parties helps to solidify your reputation as the urban tribe *social chair.*

Now there's nothing wrong with a few random roommates, coworkers, or visiting cousins suddenly showing up on the guest list because knowing your guests is a two-way street. As you begin to establish your reputation as the *social chair*, your many accolades will accompany these secondary invitations. And since your friends won't want to disappoint that random roommate, coworker, or visiting cousin, they'll most likely be sure to give you a heads-up about any specific dietary restrictions or party preferences.

We are always straightforward with you, and we will be honest: Our vision of the perfect party starts with the guest list and radiates out to the menu, signature cocktail, activities, and decorations. But we also must note that we have some pretty cool friends, which makes this technique work. So if your friends don't make this technique work, get new ones. Really.

ST. VALENTINE'S DAY MASSACRE

Just because you know the holiday was invented by Hallmark,

doesn't mean you don't want flowers and presents!

CONCEPT

The ultimate in decadence. The menu is "Death by Chocolate" and the evening's activity is another *mixer* for adults. If you work it right, you can line up your date for next Valentine's Day! If you're married, seriously dating, or engaged, sorry, this party isn't for you. Go quietly and enjoy your romance elsewhere.[3] However, you'll be demanding the pictures from your single friends and speculating about the debauchery over dinner with your sweetie.

When your faithful founders were *collegiates*, one of their favorite events was called Grab-a-Date. The sorority *social chair* would advise the *sisters* to meet at a certain place at a specified time. On arrival, the *sisters* would be informed that they had 30 minutes to go out, grab a date, and meet back at the party location. While some girls would panic, Morgan

---

3. Men are pathologically afraid of Valentine's Day. So trust us, if you're in a relationship, you're going to dinner. Dinner is pretty much the only thing men know how to do in the face of their fear.

and Brooksie, even then the party time-management gurus, would spend 10 minutes lining up the appropriate group of 8 to 12 men to act as their dates and then spend the remaining 20 minutes getting their preparty drink on. Who says less is more?

Anyway, these parties were always a good time and a great way to meet people. While you may not have grabbed the man of your dreams, you could normally trade up to a guy brought to the party by another one of your *sisters*. Now, we know that you aren't still living on a college campus—at least we hope not! And since you don't live with hundreds of single men, we propose something that fits your new station in life. Plan on inviting six other women. Have each female party guest bring two pretend boyfriends for an evening of mixing with single women. (Don't know what a pretend boyfriend is? See "A Word About . . ." at the end of this party). That's right, the hostess invites only other girls and each female guest and the hostess is responsible for inviting two single guys and bringing a chocolate dessert of her own creation. No guest or hostess should invite a guy she herself is interested in. Instead, invite guys who, although lovely, have been removed from your personal romantic candidate list. That way, neither you nor the guys feel encumbered or unable to mingle.

Recycling—it's not just for environmentalists anymore!

DECORATIONS

Two single men per single female in the room
1 stock card per male guest to be made into
    the invitation
25 white tea lights
10 candles per 1,500 square feet of party
    space
1 string of 100 white Christmas tree lights
    per 1,500 square feet of party space
30 red paper or plastic dessert plates
40 white cocktail napkins
30 sets of plastic cutlery
20 red paper cups for hot beverages
10 white wineglasses or plastic cups

Most women know whether or not they'll have a date for Valentine's Day by February 1, so time your first teaser e-mail to coincide with that date. You'll be preying on already distressed emotions, so you need to strike the appropriate balance between distaste for this card store holiday with the everlasting romantic hope we all have from watching too many John

Hughes movies in our youth. Start with a subject line such as "Are you ready for the St. Valentine's Day Massacre?" Then include the date, time, and location in the text, but only hint at what will be required of your female guests with a phrase such as "BYO(P)B**" and then translate at the bottom "Bring Your Own Pretend Boyfriends."

In the RSG world, the preferred ratio is at least two men to every female, but at minimum, you need one to one for this party sizzle. If there is any confusion about the definition of a pretend boyfriend, include Brooksie's "A Word About" in the female guests' invitations.

The next step draws from another of your founders' most revered *collegiate* traditions—the crush party. Several weeks prior to this event, the *social chair* would solicit a list of names and addresses of the men on which each *sister* had a crush. The *social committee* would proceed to distribute invitations for the crush party to the crushees, leaving most of them clueless as to who had a crush on him. For this postcollege soiree, your female friends become your committee and they must give a handwritten invitation to each pretend boyfriend they plan to bring.

Using your stock cards, write on the front, St. Valentine's Day Massacre. On the inside, list the time, date, and location. Also don't forget to add a brief explanation of the event such as, "You are cordially invited to enjoy Valentine's Day with a fine selection of chocolate, liqueur, and ladies." Most important, list your name and telephone number as the RSVP contact.

The handwritten invitation serves several purposes. First and foremost, it clarifies that this is indeed a real social event. Only one thing scares men more than planning Valentine's Day with a girlfriend: planning Valentine's Day without hope for companionship. Men, just like women, rapidly become more disgusted at the thought of spending Valentine's Day alone as February 14 gets closer. Offering them an alternative that includes lots of single women and liqueur should sound like an intriguing option. But more important, for you, our dear *rushee*, the invitation will require these men to RSVP their intentions to you so you will know how much coffee and liqueur to purchase. You should also use the conversation to make sure they know how to find the party. Remember, the men are your decorations! If you don't have them at your party, what will six of your closest girlfriends have to stare at and comment on?

Should you host this party a second year in a row, your *sisters* will have the routine down pat. They'll be scouring the city for new pretend boyfriends to bring before the invitations are even sent.

As we said before, nothing decorates a Valentine's Day party space like an array of available men. They'll arrive at 9 P.M. or whenever you tell them the party starts. Seriously, the approach is that simplistic. Set your mood with lighting. Think nightclub, but not in the strobe light kind of way, just indirect and dim. You will need tea lights, candles, and one string of white Christmas tree lights. No harsh lighting! Not even in the kitchen or the bathroom.

Now you're asking, "Can it really be this easy?" Yes, it can, and it should. What else are you going to do? Tape a bunch of paper hearts to the walls? The idea is to take the pressure off you and all your single friends. You are doing a public service here. If more people shared their pretend boyfriends with their friends in this manner, there would be far fewer singles getting uncomfortable e-mails from strangers reading their profiles on an online dating service. Quit stressing about the fact it's Valentine's Day and you are not currently romantically involved. Instead of feeling awkward and self-conscious about a society that believes "it takes two to make a thing go right," know your friends will think you are the coolest for presenting this sophisticated Valentine's alternative.

FOOD

The party starts at 9 P.M., so this is straight drinks and desserts. As the theme is "Death by Chocolate," each female guest should also be instructed to bring a small portion of their own chocolate creation. White chocolate, milk, dark, chocolate-raspberry, chocolate and nuts, those new reduced-carb candy truffles, whatever—encourage your guests to strive to represent the full chocolate spectrum. In chocolate as with men, variety is the spice of life. You as hostess will provide the evening's centerpiece, Take-Another-Little-Piece-of-My-Heart Tarts.

MENU

Take-Another-Little-Piece-of-My-Heart Tarts
Whatever desserts your female guests bring
Coffee, whipped cream, and Liqueur Bar
Chardonnay or other white wine

For up to 20 guests

Take-Another-Little-Piece-of-My-Heart Tarts

Two 1.4-ounce packages sugar-free, fat-free instant chocolate pudding
1 quart fat-free milk
Two 8-ounce packages fat-free Cool Whip–type whipped topping
Three 8-ounce packages 8 small tart crusts
One 16-ounce or smaller package frozen raspberries (at least 24 raspberries)
One 16-ounce or smaller package frozen blueberries (at least 24 blueberries)

This tart with fat-free chocolate mousse filling is so simple to make, you'll have lots of time to do your hair and makeup.

In a bowl large enough to hold the 1 quart of milk and the 16 ounces of fat-free whipped topping, mix together the pudding mix and milk. Whisk until the pudding begins to set. Next stir in the whipped topping, folding in 4 ounces at a time so that the pudding and the whipped topping are completely mixed. Place the pudding/whipped topping mix in the refrigerator to set for about 2 hours. While your tart filling is in the refrigerator, bake your tart shells, following the instructions on the package, and then set them aside to cool. Thaw the berries. After the tart shells have cooled and the tart filling has set, scoop the tart filling into the cooled tart shells. Do not overfill, just fill up to the crust line. Sprinkle a few thawed berries in the center. Makes 24 tarts.

Coffee and Liqueur Bar

Now, for the drinks. As the book title says, *Men Are from Mars, Women Are from Venus*. Your faithful founders suggest you take this to heart and provide separate beverage options for the sexes. A coffee bar complete with a small selection of liqueurs and whipped cream will provide your male guests with the perfect combination of caffeine and liquid courage.

8 ounces of coffee (see Note below)
½ gallon of milk (for coffee)
1 cup sugar (for coffee)
One 14-ounce can fat-free whipped cream
One 750-ml bottle Irish whiskey
One 750-ml bottle Bailey's Irish Cream
One 750-ml bottle Kahlùa, Amaretto, or Frangelico

Simply brew a pot of coffee and transfer it to an attractive thermal carafe. Present it on a kitchen counter or at the end of your food table with the liqueurs, milk, sugar, and the can of whipped cream. Check coffee periodically and brew more as needed.

Note: 1 pound of coffee yields forty conventional cups. Since the drinks you are serving, are half liqueur and half coffee, you should only need one pound to adequately serve your guests.

White Wine

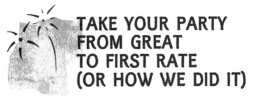

1 case white wine (Chardonnay or wine of your choice)

For the women, we recommend white wine. We've never met a woman who didn't enjoy her Chardonnay[4] and start to loosen up after that third glass. You'll need relaxed, chatty women for this party to really work. Besides, serving one kind of wine allows you to buy in volume and get the all-important per case discount, which can be up to 15 percent at some stores.

MAKE THE MOOD COME ALIVE

What could be better than a CD mix of antilove anthems that then shifts into more romantic territory? Start with J. Geils "Love Stinks" and take it from there. After all it is Valentine's Day and attending this party means you don't have a Valentine—yet. But as the sparks start to fly, transition the music to fit the level of flirting. After two potential couples have provided poorly constructed excuses to leave early, it's time to put on "Wonderful Tonight" and blow out a few candles.

Again we cannot stress how crucial the dim lighting is for this party. In addition to making everyone more attractive, the elongated shadows will create hiding spots for potential couples to share some stolen moments away from prying eyes.

TAKE YOUR PARTY FROM GREAT TO FIRST RATE (OR HOW WE DID IT)

Add a party favor. Purchase two large bags of the candy hearts with messages written on them. Not only are they theme-appropriate, the candies themselves are fat-free. Transfer them to small candy bags, found in most craft stores,

---

4. Whenever possible, the Society of Recovering Sorority Girls encourages their members and *rushees* to buy and drink American! So when we say Chardonnay we mean California. Possibly Washington. Maybe a winery local to your home state.

tie with red curling ribbon, and distribute them as party favors.

Purchase a dozen red roses to create several smaller groupings. Place the smaller bouquets in the bathroom, on the coffee table, and in the kitchen. It hints of romance and provides a beautiful aroma.

Play spin the bottle. Yes, it's silly and screams seventh grade boy-girl party, but you'll be surprised by how much fun adults can have playing. The difference most likely correlates to the percentage of adults who wear braces as opposed to the percentage of seventh graders who wear braces.

TIMELINE

Two weeks before the party—Send your e-mail to your girlfriends and begin handwriting invitations for the men. As your goal is two guys per girl and optimal party size is twenty, invite six other girls, figuring that one won't come up with her two.

Ten days before the party—Make sure your girlfriends are handing out the invitations to their pretend boyfriends.

One week before the party—Have your hair trimmed and highlighted if necessary.

Two days before the party—Finalize your guest list.

The evening before the party—Tidy the party space, perform any beauty rituals that could result in temporary redness or irritation.

The morning of the party—Purchase dessert ingredients, coffee, liqueurs, wine, and paper goods. Chill the Chardonnay.

6:30 P.M.	Make the tart filling; set in the refrigerator. Bake the tart shells; set to cool. Thaw the berries.
6:45 P.M.	String the white Christmas tree lights and place the candles where you want them.
7:45 P.M.	Finish your hair and makeup.
8:30 P.M.	Prepare the tarts.
8:45 P.M.	Brew the first pot of coffee.
8:50 P.M.	Light the candles.
9 P.M.	Greet the guests as they arrive.

A WORD ABOUT . . . PRETEND BOYFRIENDS

This is Brooksie here, and I can tell you that it's not easy being single in your late twenties. When you don't have a date, you feel like everyone else does, and no matter how strong and independent you are, or how great your new hair color looks, going to the movies alone on a Friday night is still a little intimidating. Enter the pretend boyfriend.

The pretend boyfriend is a nice guy with whom you are friends but have no romantic sparks. He's your stand-in date for weddings; he will help you set up your computer and most important, he's there for you when you need a pretend date like dinner and a movie. Sure, it's not as much fun as a real date as you won't get nervous wondering if he's a good kisser or not. But it sure beats sitting at home watching *Trading Spaces*. Plus, when you do have a real boyfriend and need a translation of guy-speak, your pretend boyfriend is looking out for you, and he'll tell you if the real boyfriend is of his caliber, or just another dog unworthy of your sparkling presence.

Now that you know what a pretend boyfriend is, let's just clarify what does not count as a pretend boyfriend. A pretend boyfriend is *not* someone you have a crush on but who refers to you as, "Hey, you, in payroll." A pretend boyfriend is *not* an ex-boyfriend. A pretend boyfriend is a guy friend who treats you well, but someone you will not sleep with because it's simply never seemed like a good idea at any time—not even the night involving those tequila shots after someone who is thirty-

five and still called Skipper got promoted to the job you really wanted.

If the women who are invited bring anyone other than pretend boyfriends to your party, it will fail. An ex, no matter how amiable the breakup, will spark feelings of jealousy. And if a guy a woman has a crush on starts hitting on her best friend, she'll be overcome by Valentine's Day–inspired rage. Neither option is good; in fact, they both sound like big buzz kills. Sticking with a pretend boyfriend is a good idea, because if things work out for him at this party, his "date" will be the coolest girl in the world to him, and he's guaranteed to always help her do yucky things in life, like move her and all her furniture into that fourth-floor walk-up.

ENTERTAINING-STYLE QUIZ

Our dear *rushees*! There's no reason to feel overwhelmed by all the great party ideas. This quiz is scientifically designed to help you decide which parties to incorporate into your social calendar.

1. If you were a color you would be:
   a. Fuchsia.
   b. Provence yellow.
   c. Basic black.
   d. Sky blue.
   e. Beige.

2. Your favorite song is:
   a. "Margaritaville."
   b. "I Still Haven't Found What I'm Looking For."
   c. "The Way You Look Tonight."
   d. "Don't You Forget About Me."
   e. "Mmm Bop."

3. When at a bar waiting for a friend you order:
   a. Cheap domestic beer.
   b. Cheap domestic white wine.
   c. A cosmo—top shelf.
   d. A cosmo—lower shelf.
   e. Caffeine-free Diet Coke.

4. It's noon on Friday. Your friend calls to cancel your dinner plans. What do you do?
    a. Call your twenty other friends to go hang at the new hot dance spot.
    b. Call your roommate and propose dinner and a movie out.
    c. Call that bouncer you know and get VIP passes to the sold-out club show. Make the friend who canceled green with envy during Saturday dinner as you discuss your antics with Mikey the drummer.
    d. Ask the cute guy in the office next to you to grab coffee and take in a reading at your local yuppie hot spot.
    e. Feel relieved. Now you can continue to catalog your sock drawer.

5. What is your favorite TV show?
    a. MTV's *Real World* (Especially the Las Vegas season—you can *do* that on TV?)
    b. *Friends.*
    c. Whatever is playing on the TV over the bar.
    d. Quiz show.
    e. The news.

6. What is your idea of a truly great vacation?
    a. Partying in Cancun. Two words: swim-up bar.
    b. Road trip with the girls to some offbeat historical sights.
    c. Wandering the beaches and museums of Italy with your new "friend" Paolo.
    d. Twenty-two cities—eighteen days—fifty-four people—one bus.
    e. There's no place like home!

7. Describe the majority of the shoes that you have owned:

    a. Platforms.

    b. Candie's slides.

    c. Strappy sandals with dangerously high heels.

    d. Neutral pumps with a business-appropriate heel.

    e. Sensible.

8. Describe your dream car:

    a. Convertible Jeep Wrangler.

    b. Volkswagen Jetta.

    c. BMW Convertible Roadster (When the limo driver is unavailable . . .).

    d. Honda Accord.

    e. Toyota Camry.

9. Describe your dating style:

    a. To paraphrase SR 71, you may not be Mr. Right, but you'll do right now.

    b. Dating around.

    c. Dating several of the most eligible bachelors in town.

    d. Steady Eddie.

    e. Dating? But my brother Stu takes me everywhere I want to go!

10. What was your major?

    a. Undeclared. (It's so hard to decide what you like when you never go to class.)

    b. Business Administration.

    c. Liberal Arts.

    d. Accounting.

    e. Dual major—Quantum Physics/Network Systems Applications.

11. Who do you most admire?

    a. Karen Walker from TV's *Will and Grace*.
    b. The First Lady.
    c. Marilyn Monroe.
    d. Mother Teresa.
    e. Your eighth-grade algebra teacher.

If you answered mostly **A's**, your party style is: *Pledge*

You have a cup in one hand and the address of the rugby house in the other. Mom and Dad have *no idea* what you are up to. You've been at school for 2 weeks, but you've yet to make it to a single class. As an adult, when you're not planning the next office happy hour, you're busy combing the city for the Next Big Thing. Your friends always have a good time with you, but claim you can be "too much fun." You would enjoy the Cabin Fever Beach Party, Mardi Gras Party, Cinco de Mayo, and the End-of-Summer Pool Party.

If you answered mostly **B's**, your party style is: *Sister*.

You had your wild phase, but you tend to be a little more reserved now. You still know how to have a good time, but you've given up drinking in quantity for drinking in quality and don't mind spending a few extra bucks. You would enjoy New Martini's Eve, St. Patrick's Day Pub Party, the Italian Street Festival, and *Beaujolais Nouveau Est Arrivé*.

If you answered mostly **C's**, your party style is: *Social Chair*.

You do *everything* fabulously. A simple night out turns into an adventure you'll be able to tell your grandchildren about. Your *sisters* voted you "Most Likely to Date a Rock Star" and you're still not exactly sure where that tattoo came from. You would enjoy the St. Valentine's Day Massacre, Kentucky Derby, Columbus Day Party (or how to turn any old day into an excuse to celebrate), and December's Black Tie and Tiara Informal Formal.

If you answered mostly **D's,** your party style is: *Risk Management.*

You know that there is a time and a place for everything. You like to have fun, but all that loud music gives you a headache. What used to be your party clothes now feel tight and binding. If you can't do it in khakis and a white Gap T-shirt, it's probably not worth doing. You would enjoy the Chinese New Year's Party, Red-Hot Fourth of July Potluck, Tailgate to Touchdown, and Halloween Party II.

If you answered mostly **E's,** your party style is: *Cut from Rush.*

You don't have a moment to lose and thank God you bought this book, because, honey, you need a fun makeover. Frankly, if you'd had one back in the day, you might have gotten a *bid* during sorority *rush*. You might not enjoy any of the parties, but you really do need to throw them. Trust us. Perhaps you don't think you can get enough guests for a high-quality guest list. One word: Coworkers. If you follow our directions, step by step, you might actually be able to successfully host: the Japanese Cherry Blossom Festival, the Ultimate Road Trip, and Christmas Chaos Covered.

Chapter Three

MARCH

MARDI GRAS PARTY

Beads, Beignets, and Bon Temps!

CONCEPT

Laissez les bons temps rouler! A bonus of entering the recovering stage of life is that you're too sophisticated to spend your time jammed elbow to elbow with thousands of other people while you wait in line for a Porta-Potty on Bourbon Street. But do we ever outgrow shiny plastic beads? Now that you are throwing the party, you won't even need to flash to get 'em—unless you want to!

Although the most famous American Mardi Gras celebration is in New Orleans, the grand tradition of pre-Lenten carnival is celebrated in great style throughout the world, notably in Nice, Rio, and Cologne. The celebration of Mardi Gras as a last blast before the personal sacrifice of Lent can be traced back to the Middle Ages. Now, however, Mardi Gras is more an expression of secular hedonism, and all of the messy preparation for self-sacrifice can be ignored. So, if you can't get to Rio or, better yet, to Cologne, bring New Orleans into your living room through savvy Internet shopping and treat your nearest and dearest to good food, good fun, and cheap plastic beads!

Mardi Gras typically falls between February 3 and March 9, but you have some flexibility with the dates. It's really more of a mood than a specific day. Modern Mardi Gras in New Orleans began in the 1700s. The festival takes the form of twelve days of parades leading up to the grand finale on the Tuesday before Lent. Individual parades and parade floats are sponsored by private organizations known as Krewes.

Interestingly, the official cocktail of Mardi Gras, the hurricane, did not make an appearance until World War II. Folklore has it that legendary New Orleans restaurateur Pat O'Brien developed the drink in response to

DECORATIONS

400 strands of assorted inexpensive beads

15 sheets of gold, purple, and green construction paper (5 pieces of each color)

1 keg of purple curling ribbon

1 keg of green curling ribbon

1 black Magic Marker

1 roll of Scotch tape

30 gold paper or plastic plates

30 gold paper or plastic bowls

40 gold napkins

30 sets of plastic cutlery in green or purple

40 purple or green plastic or paper cups

wartime liquor restrictions. At that time, rum was plentiful while other liquors were scarce. O'Brien, faced with an overflow of rum, did what Morgan and Brooksie would have done in the face of adversity: he found an ultratasty use for it, giving birth to the hurricane!

Think gold, green, and purple, the signature colors of an authentic "Nawlins" Mardi Gras. On sheets of appropriately colored construction paper write the names of various Krewes and parades to set the mood. Not familiar with Mardi Gras? Don't worry, we've got you covered with Krewe and parade names on page 50. The kitchen can be Orpheus, the balcony Zulu. Why not? Remember to alternate colored backgrounds and don't forget to decorate the bathroom(s)! The colors are de rigueur for Mardi Gras.

Apply your fabulous Chinese New Year's Party experience and give your party space the curling ribbon treatment! Alternating the colors, hit that chandelier, food table, coffee table, end table, stemware, banister—and don't forget those doorknobs.

The main event for decorations and also for your party activity is the beads. Mardi Gras beads are widely available via every RSG's best friend: Internet shopping. Got a few spare minutes at work? Log on and comparison shop for some beads. Just type Mardi Gras Beads in any search engine and the choices that come up will seem endless. The colors, shapes, and styles are equally varied.

You can get a two-hundred-strand value pack set of single colored strands for between $15 and $30 per pack. We recommend that you get at least two. Set aside at least two hundred strands for your guests to wear and trade and use the majority of the second pack as decorations. You can tie the strands together to make a garland, doubling the effect of your curling ribbon, for a truly festive scene.

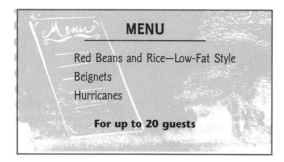

MENU

Red Beans and Rice—Low-Fat Style

Beignets

Hurricanes

For up to 20 guests

Red Beans and Rice—Low-Fat Style

Red Beans and Rice are a venerable New Orleans tradition. This version replaces the fatty pork sausage and gets away from the lard and the oil to create a tasty dish the boys will love without threatening your ability to fit into that cute skirt you've been eyeing.

4 cups water

32 ounces low-sodium, fat-free chicken broth

1 tablespoon plus 1 teaspoon cayenne pepper

1 tablespoon plus 1 teaspoon cumin

1 tablespoon plus 1 teaspoon thyme

2 teaspoons dry mustard

2 teaspoons chili powder

2 teaspoons black pepper

1 teaspoon dried oregano

4 cups jasmine rice

Three 26-ounce cans light red kidney beans, drained

2 pounds turkey smoked sausage

In a large, sturdy pot mix together 4 cups water, the chicken broth, spices, rice, and drained kidney beans. Remove the turkey smoked sausage from the package, cut the sausage into rounds approximately 1/4 inch thick, and then cut the rounds into quarters. Add the sausage pieces to the pot. Heat the ingredients over high heat to boiling and then simmer, covered, on low heat for 20 minutes, stirring occasionally.

Beignets

Normally, your faithful founders would never counsel you to serve any member of the doughnut family, but they don't call it "Fat Tuesday" for nothing! There are two choices here. Choice one:

Make your own batter. That, however, just seems too messy. Instead, take choice two: Get yourself some Café du Monde Beignet mix, either at your local grocery or by Internet mail order.

**Two 28-ounce boxes of Café du Monde
   Beignet mix**
**3 cups canola oil if pan-frying (use oil as directed
   on package if using a deep-fryer)**
Powdered sugar for dusting beignets

Follow the directions on the package and then, and we will *never* use this phrase again, deep-fry the dough. Finish with a dusting of powdered sugar just before you are ready to serve them.

Hurricanes

For a signature cocktail there is no choice but the hurricane. There are many schools of thought on correct preparation. Some are ridiculous, such as a Bacardi premade that is blue, and a British version that uses two types of rum, gin, and Amaretto and sounds like stomach distress just waiting to happen. Others, however, are sublime like the original, Pat O'Brien's mix, yours for $12.99 per gallon, not including the cost of the rum. Many recipes call for the use of both light and dark rum in each drink. But as Morgan's friend Cheryl said after

an emergency room trip induced by such a preparation, "The doctor says, never mix light and dark rum." So, on the advice of our medical expert, Morgan's-friend-Cheryl's-doctor, we make the bold recommendation to go dark. Not Myers's Rum dark—think Captain Morgan dark. This approach creates a light, yet fruity taste treat, not unlike Kool-Aid for adults.

**Two 1.75-liter bottles dark rum, preferably
   Captain Morgan Original Spiced Rum**
One 32-ounce bottle lime juice
**1 quart reduced-calorie orange juice
   (see Note for more information)**
One 25-ounce bottle Rose's Grenadine
1 cup Splenda
3 oranges, unpeeled, sliced thinly into rounds
One 10-ounce jar Maraschino cherries

Combine punch-bowl style, 1 liter and 6 ounces of the dark rum, 1¼ cups of the lime juice, 1¼ cups of the orange juice, 1¼ cups grenadine, and ⅓ cup Splenda. Toss in some orange slices and maraschino cherries. You'll have about 20 hurricanes to enjoy, so keep the recipe handy—it will make two more rougly equal batches. This is the recipe to make 20 hurricanes. Party math dictates 60 are needed for 20 guests, but it's very difficult to mix all 60 at once.

Note: Feel free to use calcium-enriched orange juice. It doesn't affect the flavor and calcium encourages weight loss and protects bone density!

MAKE THE MOOD COME ALIVE

It's time to go to the library or cruise the sale rack at your local record store. New Orleans is a city of music. Good choices are Cajun Zydeco bands, the Preservation Hall Jazz Band, and Dixieland jazz. If you are really looking to score points for authenticity, find "If Ever I Cease to Love," the traditional Mardi Gras anthem adopted by the Krewe of Rex.

The traditional, but with a twist, Cajun menu, the decorations, and the hurricanes carry your mood far, but the real star is the beads. Upon arrival give each guest an array of at least ten strands of beads to wear. Purchase several specialty strands to mix in and encourage your guests to barter with one another for the beads that they want. This encourages conversation and party flow!

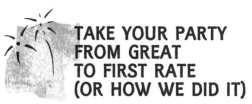

TAKE YOUR PARTY FROM GREAT TO FIRST RATE (OR HOW WE DID IT)

While parade goers in the French Quarter are bombarded with colorful decorations and throws from revelers atop wrought-iron balconies overlooking Bourbon Street, for your home create a similar upward visual interest. A simple crepe paper canopy will evoke that French Quarter feel. You will need either a Styrofoam or metal ring approximately 12 inches in diameter to hang from the center of the ceiling of the main-party-space room. Using three colors of crepe paper—gold, purple, and green—attach alternating streamers to the ring, twist the streamers party style, and attach them to the corresponding wall. The streamer should bow slightly in the middle, accenting your canopy. However, it should not dip so low that your tallest guest will be ducking underneath it all night.

But for the most important first-rate touch we have only two words: King Cake. The King Cake appears to be a member of the coffee cake family. We have been told, by people with time enough to undertake it, that if you make the King Cake from scratch, it can take up to 8 hours. No self-respecting *rushee* or member of

Rho Sigma Gamma has that kind of time to spend on a ritual that is not beauty-related! So don't bake it, buy it. Many Gulf Coast bakeries will FedEx you an authentic King Cake at reasonable rates. As the cakes are not delicate pastry they hold up quite well in the mail. The cake is a great tradition and makes a fabulous centerpiece for your table. Everyone enjoys trying to find the good luck plastic baby baked into the ring-shaped cake. Tradition dictates that the lucky party guest who gets the baby in his or her piece of cake must provide next year's King Cake.

Finally, party favors. Although you have beads, beads, beads, mail-order New Orleans pralines are a great touch to give to your guests on their way out.

TIMELINE

To establish your timeline, first you must set the date of your party. Although Mardi Gras is a 12-day affair, we only expect you to pick one night. For most people, the Saturday night before Fat Tuesday is often the best date.

Three weeks before the party—Send your e-mail invitation, order your beads, beignet mix, and if you are taking your party from great to first-rate, the King Cake.

One week before the party—The beads and the beignet mix have arrived. Purchase the remaining decorations, plates, bowls, cups, and utensils. Make entertainment decisions and procure the music.

The day before the party—Make your trip to the grocery store and liquor store. You may want to make a single portion of your hurricane recipe, just to make sure you like the way it tastes. Give yourself a lip mask, because as Brooksie can attest, one of Cologne's Carnivale traditions is to collect kisses. And in late winter, your lips may be shockingly dry!

The morning of the party—Time to tidy up. As Morgan likes to say, just running the vacuum over the carpet can fool people into thinking you actually cleaned the place. Wait for FedEx to bring your King Cake. Start hanging those beads and curling ribbon. This will take some time, because creating a veritable French Quarter in your party space is not a process that can be done in a rush, nor should it. Just put on some of that great Cajun Zyedco music you got last Saturday and get to it!

The afternoon of the party—Take your preparty nap. Mardi Gras can be an exhausting affair!

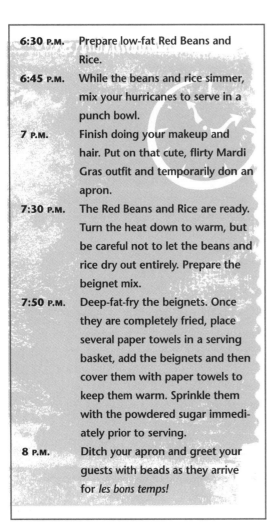

6:30 P.M.	Prepare low-fat Red Beans and Rice.
6:45 P.M.	While the beans and rice simmer, mix your hurricanes to serve in a punch bowl.
7 P.M.	Finish doing your makeup and hair. Put on that cute, flirty Mardi Gras outfit and temporarily don an apron.
7:30 P.M.	The Red Beans and Rice are ready. Turn the heat down to warm, but be careful not to let the beans and rice dry out entirely. Prepare the beignet mix.
7:50 P.M.	Deep-fat-fry the beignets. Once they are completely fried, place several paper towels in a serving basket, add the beignets and then cover them with paper towels to keep them warm. Sprinkle them with the powdered sugar immediately prior to serving.
8 P.M.	Ditch your apron and greet your guests with beads as they arrive for *les bons temps!*

A WORD ABOUT . . . MARDI GRAS PARADES

As we all know, Mardi Gras is a twelve-day-long celebration of all things decadent, leading up to its climax on Fat Tuesday. During Mardi Gras there are a series of parades and each parade features floats sponsored by organizations called Krewes. Your faithful founders admire Krewes because they have much in common with Greek organizations. Like fraternities and sororities, Krewes trace their origins to the middle-part of nineteenth-century America. The first Krewe was called the Mystick Krewe of Comus and was founded in 1857. Krewes are private, usually single-sex organizations and not only do they sponsor parades and build floats, they sponsor balls! So naturally, we have great affection for them.

Parades and Krewes have varying degrees of prestige and honor and in most cases have their own colors and emblems. Most Krewes and parades operate their own Internet sites, which can be put to good use in procuring decorations. A short and generalized list of parades and corresponding Krewes is presented here in alphabetical order.

The Krewe of Babylon is one of the ten oldest parading Krewes in the City of New

Orleans. Secrecy is a trademark of this Krewe; the identity of their king is never released to the general public and the exact title of their parade and ball theme are not disclosed until the day of the event.

A latecomer to the scene, the Krewe of Bacchus aimed to bring national attention to Mardi Gras with its gigantic floats and Hollywood celebrities as king. The Krewe of Bacchus began in 1969, but is well regarded as one of the "super krewes" of Carnival.

The Krewe of Comus, originally named the Mystick Krewe of Comus, was founded in 1857, making it the oldest Krewe to originally parade. In 1992, the Krewe of Comus refused to sign a city ordinance prohibiting racial discrimination among the Krewes and withdrew from the parade schedule.

The Krewe of Iris is now New Orleans' sole parading Carnival organization exclusively for women and the largest ladies' club in Carnival history. Founded in 1917, it is named for the goddess of the rainbow and messenger to the gods.

The Krewe of Orpheus was founded in 1993, but its first parade had over seven hundred members. The Krewe throws three different types of doubloons and features flambeaux, stilt walkers, and several marching bands.

The Phunny Phorty Phellows celebrates the official opening of Mardi Gras season by riding a decorated streetcar along St. Charles Avenue. Since 1981, the Heralds of Mardi Gras have dined on King Cakes and sipped champagne while tossing throws to the spectators.

Rex made its debut in 1872 and is quite possibly the international symbol of New Orleans Mardi Gras. This Krewe began the tradition of the King of Carnival, who arrives on a yacht. They also introduced the colors of Mardi Gras—purple, gold, and green. Organizers of the first daytime parade, it remains the main event of Mardi Gras day.

Founded in 1909, and first parading in 1914, the Zulu Social Aid and Pleasure Club is the second-oldest African-American Krewe and the oldest African-American Krewe on the parade schedule. Zulu is said to have begun as a parody of Rex, but it is now composed of many prominent community leaders. This parade boasts one of the most distinctive throws, the prized golden nuggets or coconuts.

ST. PATRICK'S DAY
PUB PARTY

Because green beer will only stain your carpet

and clash with your makeup!

CONCEPT

Just because you don't have time to travel to Ireland to celebrate St. Patrick's Day doesn't mean you can't have a good time celebrating Irish culture. We recommend breaking away from shamrocks and leprechauns. Instead celebrate a modern and more realistic Ireland. So let go of the Ireland found on cereal boxes and in soap commercials and celebrate the Ireland of "Junior Year Abroad"—turn your home into an Irish pub!

If you've never been to Ireland, you're probably thinking, "Irish pub—are you mad? My home is nice! Why would I want to transform it into a bar?" Relax, it's O.K., because an Irish pub is almost the complete opposite of an American bar! As good sorority girls, we believe the Irish pub is the cultural equivalent of the fraternity/sorority *mixer*. Only instead of the *sisters* meeting and greeting with the *brothers*, it's a place where community members and wayward travelers share a drink, a story, and perhaps a song. No pretenses, no expectations, just a good time with your friends and new acquaintances. The fact that you will be re-creating that atmosphere in your living room makes this party perfect in a calm and subdued way. If you're still confused, please read A Word About, at the end of this chapter.

DECORATIONS

1 large rectangular blackboard

An assortment of cardboard bar coasters

1 dartboard and 4 dart sets

An assortment of Irish liquor advertisements

4 printouts of soccer or Irish rugby schedules

40 green, white, or orange napkins

30 green, white, or orange paper or plastic plates

40 green, white, or orange plastic cups

1 green and 1 orange cloth, vinyl, or paper tablecloths for your food-serving area

30 sets of plastic cutlery

1 package of colored chalk

Your decorations are not decorations as much as they are an attitude.[1] First and foremost is the blackboard. Every Irish pub worth its salt has a chalkboard list of the day's spe-

cials and prices. You can re-create that with fictional prices for your traditional, yet delicious, menu.

Also, to set the mood, pub coasters are available at most housewares stores. Other classic touches include a dartboard, liquor ads, and soccer or Irish rugby schedules. (The Internet can be a valuable resource in this regard). Display each schedule prominently throughout your party space and don't forget the bathrooms. Use extra care when selecting the location of the dartboard. It should be in the main pub area but should not make a trip to the food table a life-threatening endeavor.

Just because we have forbidden shiny green shamrocks, doesn't mean we are abandoning the green of the Irish hills or the white and the orange, which complete the tricolor flag. Use these three colors to round out any gaps in terms of napkins, plates, cups, tablecloths, etc.

FOOD

Take a rain check on traditional fare like corned beef and cabbage or fish and chips. They'll just make your house smell bad! We

---

1. Under no circumstances should you use shiny green shamrock anything! Leprechauns will hunt you down and hurt you if you do.

have cobbled together this "pub grub" menu from our beer-soaked memories of study abroad.

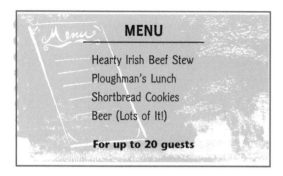

MENU

Hearty Irish Beef Stew
Ploughman's Lunch
Shortbread Cookies
Beer (Lots of It!)

For up to 20 guests

Hearty Irish Beef Stew

16 small to medium Yukon Gold potatoes

Six 14-ounce cans low sodium, reduced fat
    beef broth

Two 14.9-ounce cans Guinness

2 teaspoons dry mustard

4 tablespoons Worcestershire sauce

Dash of salt

4 teaspoons black pepper

2 medium onions

One 8-ounce package of baby carrots

4 pounds lean stewing beef

1 tablespoon olive oil per batch of beef

½ teaspoon fresh crushed garlic per batch
    of beef

2 tablespoons fresh parsley

To make the stew, the most stressful portion will be the chopping. First, chop the potatoes into large, bite-sized pieces. In a very large stew pot or crock-pot, combine the beef broth, Guinness, potatoes, dry mustard, Worcestershire sauce, salt, and pepper. Set for medium heat and simmer, covered, for at least an hour. While the potatoes simmer, chop the onions, carrots, and beef.

In a skillet or other sauté pan, heat one tablespoon of olive oil and the garlic. Once the oil sizzles, add as much of the beef as your pan will accommodate and brown it for about 5 minutes over medium heat. Be very careful not to completely cook the beef cubes, as doing so will lead to tough beef, reminiscent of the cuisine of the vile English.

Add your carrots, onion pieces, and all of the browned beef to the potatoes and broth, then simmer for an additional hour or until your potato chunks are tender and appetizing. Before serving, add the chopped parsley for color. It may look bland, but that's how the Irish like it. However, don't be fooled, we've added pepper and garlic to please your sophisticated palate, so you will find this stew very yummy.

Ploughman's Lunch

Ploughman's Lunch is a traditional Irish specialty. Although the recipe usually includes a pickled egg, we've omitted it because we don't like stinky food. Instead, just concentrate on the bread, cheese, and beer portions.

Three 1-pound loaves of Irish brown bread
2 pounds assorted cheeses

Specifically, we recommend making four separate platters of nicely arranged, hearty slices of Irish brown bread and the assorted cheeses. Guests who wish to transfer portions of the platter onto their own plates should be counseled to also take a bottle of bitter beer, i.e., a pale ale or a stout for a more authentic experience. Once you've purchased the Irish brown bread, shortbread cookies, and cheese at the grocery store, all that's left to "cook" is the stew.

Shortbread Cookies

Rushees, your tour of duty in the kitchen is now over. Complete your meal with a dessert— store-bought shortbread cookies. Three 5.3-ounce boxes should be plenty. While shortbread is more Scottish than Irish, real Irish desserts are scary![2] Scary = bad party experience, plus lots of leftovers.

Beer (Lots of It!)

For your beverage, we recommend a nice selection of Irish beers. Consult your liquor store manager for suggestions available in your area. Well-known Irish beers include Guinness, Murphy's, and Harp. Killian's is an American alternative. In a pinch, go with your favorite microbrews. Selecting a beer in Europe is like selecting a sports team to follow, a process driven by locality and fierce loyalty. Bring the European process to your party.

MAKE THE MOOD COME ALIVE

Irish pop music. Start with the subtle like Black 47, U2, the Corrs, the Cranberries, Sinéad O'Connor, Van Morrison, and the Chieftains, then end the night with great Irish sing-a-long music like the Irish Rovers. Almost every American over the age of eighteen has been to a pub somewhere singing along to "The Unicorn," and after a few pints it'll seem appropriate.

We don't expect you to have a pool table to host a major billiards competition, but a

2. Remember that episode of *Friends* when only Joey would eat Rachel's trifle?

dartboard is cheap, not to mention a professional sport in Ireland (think bowling, but foreign!) and a dart tournament is a great way to get the conversation started. However, if you notice that one of your guests has had a wee too much Irish whiskey or double digits in beers, it's probably not a good idea to give that person any type of pointy projectiles—especially if you value your pets. Instead, put your intoxicated friend to work as a "line judge." Just because someone has had too much to drink doesn't mean that person has to miss out on all the fun. It's just not the Irish or the RSG way!

Now, let's have one more word about that pool table. If you, coincidentally, have a pool table in your home, by all means, a major billiards tournament is in order. Establishing teams with your e-mail will create awesome preparty buzz, and start the party off with a bang. And if you don't invite Morgan and Brooksie, they'll talk to those leprechauns about your party faux pas.

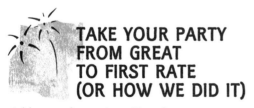

TAKE YOUR PARTY FROM GREAT TO FIRST RATE (OR HOW WE DID IT)

Add some decorations. Travel posters or even postcards in your bathrooms will keep the party in Ireland no matter where your guests might wander off to. Procure a pub mirror and hang it over your bar area. If you don't have a pub mirror, a decorative mirror in your home can be transformed by writing the name of your pub or your favorite Irish whiskey in shoe polish.

Keep your drinks in the pub. Serve your Irish beer in authentic pint glasses. Most housewares stores sell them. But if you're like most former college students, you have a collection of random glasses liberated from various drinking establishments. Use them. See if anyone notices.

Organize a dart tournament among your guests. Think teams. Think competition. Think prizes. We gave out potatoes. Yukon gold for first place, new potatoes for second place, and plain old Russet for third place. What did our guests do with their potatoes? We don't care; it was just funny to give them out.

TIMELINE

Like all set date holidays, St. Patrick's Day doesn't always fall on an ideal party night. Additionally, this is a popular American holiday that has spawned parades, festivals, and all kinds of neat local events. However, because this isn't exactly a St. Patrick's Day Party, but more of an Irish Pub Party, you have some leeway. Check your schedule and select either the Saturday before or after the seventeenth. Your timeline then counts back from that day.

Because St. Patrick's Day is popular in most communities, it's better to get your party on people's calendars sooner rather than later. You should probably start telling people about the awesome party you are planning in late February, and quickly follow up with an e-mail around the first of March.

If you lack many of the decorations outlined above, you should probably make a shopping trip the weekend before your party, so you have a full seven days to make the decorations and plan the layout of your party space. Although there aren't many decorations needed to create the pub, your party space *must* be decorated before any of your guests arrive. Otherwise, you're just a half step above a common beer bash.

The night before the party—Straighten up, and as always, move any breakables to a safer location. As with any party, it's easier to decorate a tidy party space, rather than pick up as you go along. Also, remember to complete those beauty tasks that could result in redness or irritation (exfoliation, eyebrow management,

etc.). These are rituals that require 12 hours of healing; don't shortchange yourself. Normally, we also remind you to plan your party outfit. But since you'll only be going to an Irish pub, you can easily get away with jeans and a trendy top. We know every RSG *rushee* has those.

The afternoon of the party—Go to the grocery store and visit your local beer merchant, which in some states may be one and the same.

4 P.M.	Make sure your beer is chilling.[3]
4:15 P.M.	Decorate your party space.
4:30 P.M.	Chop your potatoes.
5 P.M.	Start the potatoes in the pot. Chop the other stew veggies and beef while potatoes simmer.
5:50 P.M.	Brown the beef.
6 P.M.	Add the chopped veggies and browned beef to the potatoes. The stew begins to simmer.
6:15 P.M.	Finish your hair and makeup. Don't get fancy, think of this as a family event.
6:45 P.M.	Assemble the Ploughman's Lunch platters and the tray of shortbread cookies.

---

3. The Irish and the English tend to serve beer at room temperature. Although you are embracing the culture, there's no reason for things to get out of hand. Keep that beer at a proper American temperature.

| 7 P.M. | Greet your guests and make sure they know where the beer is. |

A WORD ABOUT . . .
IRISH PUB CULTURE

The Irish have a word for good times. It is *craic* (pronounced crack). And the chief pursuit in Irish leisure life is having a *craic*. Throughout modern Irish history, pub culture has been a consistent source of *craic*. For this party, it is your job to capture that down-home feeling of fellowship and fun. In America, people go to bars to meet people and perhaps hear a cover band playing much too loudly. In Ireland (and also in England—but who wants to talk about the English on a festive day like St. Patrick's Day?—people go to pubs to see their friends and neighbors, tell stories, and play video poker. Believe it or not, their way is actually more fun and more in line with a great home-

entertaining experience. After all, if your family reunion always took place at an establishment that sells really good beer, wouldn't you want to go? No pretenses, no performances, just good food, great beer, and Van Morrison. Bono would be proud.

TOP SHELF OR AN IDEA YOU SHOULD SHELVE?

A RANT BY BROOKSIE

As you'll probably notice, none of our parties advise you to provide an open bar. While we always provide an appropriate signature cocktail or beverage suggestion, we'll never tell you to set up an open bar, because frankly, they're evil.

Unless you have a licensed, experienced bartender pouring, providing an open bar invites some guy who's seen the movie *Cocktail* one too many times to test his "skills." While this scenario can have several different endings, none of them are favorable. Chances are he'll pour too strong and you'll find full glasses of hard liquor hiding behind every plant, sofa cushion, and garbage can in your house and/or at least one female guest will throw up on your favorite piece of furniture.

Open bars can encourage guests to "experiment." Now don't get me wrong, I'm as adventurous as the next person is, but hard liquor is not your eighth-grade science project. If you've ever mixed mimosas with gin and tonics and then tossed in a few shots of Jaeger for fun, you were probably awakened by either the need to hug the porcelain god or the sound of the train running through your head. We've all had the day-after experience, usually followed by a vow never to return to that bar, attend another bachelorette party, or go "drink for drink" with your cousin the Marine. Now, if you're a hostess, do you really want people having such a bad memory of your party that you are blamed for their condition? *Zut alors!* Of course not!

Not to mention, providing a quality open bar is expensive. You can't get away with the mini-bar bottles, nor will a single lifetime give you the opportunity to live down your reputation as being the hostess who provided the Tenley vodka in the plastic bottle and allowed her guests to see it. There's really no way to get around the expense of establishing a quality, top shelf open bar.

So minimize the damage your *rush group* can inflict on themselves and your pocketbook. A signature cocktail, such as those listed throughout the book or at www.recoveringsororitygirls.com, which requires only one hard liquor, will complement the theme of your party, keep the bartender-wannabes out of the kitchen, curtail experimentation, and probably have your guests reaching for a lower alcohol content wine or beer sooner rather than later.

Open bars? Much like fishnets, reunions, and anything with the word "flambé" in its name—it just sounds more fabulous than it really is.

Chapter Four

APRIL

JAPANESE CHERRY BLOSSOM FESTIVAL

A spring fling Asian style

CONCEPT

After a long, dreary winter, you're ready to party. This festival of flowers and fun is a great way to celebrate the arrival of spring, the fact your taxes are done, and the art of the intimate dinner party.

Why a Japanese Cherry Blossom Festival? This party tugs at the heartstrings of your faithful founders a little more than do most others. Since we've both lived in the Washington, D.C., area since college, we associate spring with cherry blossom blooms. Plus, going down to see them against the background of the Reflecting Pool and monuments was practically an excused absence from class.

While most of the parties your faithful founders love work well for large groups, this party is a smaller affair, better described as a dinner party. But forget the dining room table and chairs; this event calls for a more Japanese traditional seating arrangement, so we suggest pillows around your coffee table. Hey, we haven't forgotten that you're exhausted from doing those taxes. This party is light on formalities, but speaks to the joy that is six close friends getting together for a delicious bento box meal, a little sake, and perhaps some entertainment. Not sure what a bento box is? See "A Word About . . ." at the end of the Japanese Cherry Blossom Festival section.

DECORATIONS

Three 6-foot strands of cherry blossom garlands

6 red paper or plastic plates

12 white napkins—recycle from St. Patrick's Day Pub Party (if you gave it)

Paper lanterns—recycle from Chinese New Year's Party (if you gave it)

Bamboo mats—recycle from Chinese New Year's party (if you gave it)

Scotch tape

2 to 3 small bouquets of fresh light pink or white flowers

6 sets of cutlery or chopsticks

6 white or wood sake cups

Small clear bowl of water

Plate

Pebbles

In honor of spring, add a touch of cherry blossom pink as an accent color. Although fuchsia is great, and we normally love it, it's not quite right for this party. To add this subtle hue we're talking about, you'll want to find some cherry blossom garlands at your local craft store. Purchase enough to drape along the harsher edges of your party space, such as bookshelves and end tables.

Let's recycle and if you have any leftover red plates either from the St. Valentine's Day Massacre or Chinese New Year's Party, use them, along with any white napkins left from the St. Patrick's Pub Party.

We also recommend you reuse your paper lanterns and bamboo mats from the Chinese New Year's Party. Why so many decorations for only five guests? Because you already have them! Sure your *rush group* may have seen them before, but simply taking the time to put them up again speaks highly of your *social chair* training.

Spring is about bringing the outside indoors, so save some room in your party budget to purchase some fresh flowers. A small bouquet in the bathroom or any party space that lacks windows will add the smell of spring in an unexpected place.

Make a centerpiece using the elements of a traditional Shinto shrine. Place a small clear bowl of water in the middle of a plate that is larger than the bowl. Place pebbles around the bowl on the plate. The water symbolizes cleansing and the pebbles create the pathway needed to prepare people's minds for worship. Just wait for one of your friends to ask you about it, and everyone will be impressed with this seemingly random knowledge of Japanese culture.

FOOD

Please select one of the following three menus based on your *rush group*'s love or fear of sushi. True to culinary tradition, your three menu choices are called bento boxes.

Bento Box 1—Cell Phone Chef

Call your favorite sushi restaurant or gourmet grocer and order the sushi. Seriously, making sushi can be extremely complicated if you elect to use raw fish. We don't believe that home entertaining has to be as "do-it-yourself" as home improvement, which, coincidentally, is America's second favorite home-based hobby.[1] Who made up that silly rule about having to personally prepare a seven-course meal for a gathering to be considered a dinner party? We certainly didn't! So get out the Zagat guide and your phone and get that dinner done. After you order the sushi and pot stickers, all

you need to do is make the soup and buy the sake.

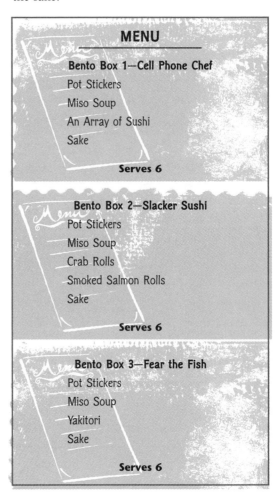

MENU

Bento Box 1—Cell Phone Chef
Pot Stickers
Miso Soup
An Array of Sushi
Sake
Serves 6

Bento Box 2—Slacker Sushi
Pot Stickers
Miso Soup
Crab Rolls
Smoked Salmon Rolls
Sake
Serves 6

Bento Box 3—Fear the Fish
Pot Stickers
Miso Soup
Yakitori
Sake
Serves 6

---

1. What's America's favorite home-based hobby? Home entertaining, of course!

Miso Soup

No restaurant-quality sushi dinner would be complete without an opening salvo of Miso Soup. While Miso Soup is not terribly difficult to make, there's no need to go overboard.

2 packages of 1.05-ounce Kikkoman
   Instant Tofu Miso Soup mix,
   enough for 1 serving per guest
1 bunch scallions, cut into ¼-inch or
   smaller round sections

Simply prepare the Miso Soup according to the instructions on the package, which generally just involves adding hot water. If for some reason, your miso mix does not include tofu or green onions, you should consider adding at least the green onions. If your guests are adverse to tofu, punch up the flavor by adding sliced shitake mushrooms instead. By adding either one, you'll fool your guests into thinking that you've secretly been dating that hunky Iron Chef, Morimoto.

Sake

Sake is a traditional Japanese beverage. In the past ten years, sake awareness has increased in the United States and recently sake bars and sake cocktails have begun to become a part of American night life. Sake is actually not wine.

It is brewed from rice, not fermented from grapes. But that is good news for budding sake enthusiasts everywhere because the rice-brewing process creates a tasty alcoholic treat without any hangover-aggravating or skin-damaging sulfites!

As the sake market has grown in America, two trends have emerged. One, Japanese sake producers, like Gekkeikan, have not been content to simply import their goods, but several have set up brewing facilities here in the United States. Second, a homegrown sake industry is taking root primarily in California, Oregon, and Colorado.

Three 750-ml bottles of sake

In general, sake can be served warm, chilled, or on the rocks. Sake experts generally set the ideal warm serving temperature at between 98 and 104 degrees. Before you decide how to serve your sake, it's important that you know your sake. Recent developments in sake-brewing technology have resulted in the creation of some newer, more aromatic sakes that are actually less flavorful if served warm. When in doubt, consult the label or that handsome guy working at your local wine shop! And if the label and the wine guy are of no help, there are some general rules of thumb. Sakes not milled below 65 percent of the original rice grain volume are good candidates for warm service. Flavor-infused sakes, like the fun and affordable Haku-san line—try the raspberry—it's delicious—are best served chilled or on the rocks.

Bento Box 2—Slacker Sushi

As we said before, raw fish is scary. If you don't know of a good sushi restaurant or if you think your guests are not big sushi fans, re-create the taste and texture of sushi using cooked imi-tation crab sticks and sushi-size slices of smoked salmon. Both of these items are available at authentic sushi restaurants as rolls, but they will not result in a 911 call in your untrained hands. Plus through minimal effort this option guaran-tees to wow your guests with a restaurant-qual-ity feast that they know was handcrafted by you!

Smoked Salmon Rolls

A helpful addition to this and the next recipe is a "sushi mat" that can be found in sushi sets or at kitchen stores. It will assist in forming beautiful rolls.

One 8-ounce package skinless smoked salmon
3 cups short grain rice or sushi rice
    (see Note for more information)
4½ cups of water
½ cup rice wine vinegar
¾ tablespoon ground ginger
2 tablespoons sugar

Cut the large pieces of smoked salmon into smaller strips that will fit neatly over the sushi rice. Your standard piece of sushi will be approximately an inch and a half in length. Think bite-size.

For sushi, especially sushi featuring fish that has already been cooked, the rice is the most important part of the preparation. Several commercial brands of sushi rice are sold in major grocery chains throughout the States. One such brand is Sushi Chef. If you have pur-chased rice designated sushi rice, follow the directions on the package to the letter. Differ-ent brands will use slightly different prepara-tions. If, however, you are sophisticated enough to select Japanese short-grain rice that is not actually labeled sushi rice and doesn't come with directions, here are the cooking basics.

Step 1, measure 3 cups of rice and put in a bowl. Rinse and mix the rice with cold water until the water runs clear. Anticipate making approximately ten rinses. Then drain in a colan-der for 1 hour. Place the drained rice in a rice cooker or in a pot with a tight-fitting lid and add 4½ cups water. Over medium heat, cover and bring the water to a boil. Boil for about 2 min-utes, and then simmer on low for about 15 min-utes. Keep the pot covered the entire time. No peeking or you'll wreck the texture! Besides, the steam escaping from the pot will let you know that your rice is cooking and will also give you a nice 15-minute steam facial. Think of it as multitasking! Once 15 minutes have passed and the steam has subsided, take the pot from the heat. Remove the pot lid and cover with a clean kitchen towel; let stand for 15 additional minutes.

While the rice cooks, combine the rice wine vinegar, ground ginger, and sugar in a small bowl, stirring until the sugar is mostly dissolved. Empty the rice into a nonmetallic dish (purists encourage the use of a "traditional flat wooden bowl"; Morgan uses a glass pie plate and it seems to work just fine), and spread it evenly over the bottom of your dish with a *shamoji*, or large wooden spoon. Run the *shamoji* through the rice in slicing motions to separate the grains. You should not be making stirring motions—only spreading and separating. After adding the separation lines, slowly add the vinegar mixture. Add only as much as is necessary. The rice should not be mushy. If you have help, fan the rice with a fan during the cooling and mixing procedures. However, the fanning step is not necessary unless you are really pressed for time.

Do not refrigerate the rice. Keep it in the dish covered with a clean cloth until ready to use. The rice will last 1 day.

Once the rice has cooled, take about a quarter of it and make into twelve 1½-inch-long bundles (saving the rest of the rice for your Crab Rolls). Place one small slice of the smoked salmon onto the rice bundles. To stop the rice from sticking to your hands, keep a bowl of water with a small amount of salt added nearby. When your hands get sticky, take a dip break. The end result is a piece of authentic-looking sushi, salmon atop a rice bundle.

Crab Rolls

For the Crab Rolls, you'll use the rest of the rice you made earlier.

One 8-ounce package stick-shaped imitation crab meat
One 1-ounce package nori (dried seaweed) containing about 10 sheets (see Note for more information)

Take your seaweed sheets and place one on a bamboo mat. Spread a very thin layer of rice onto the seaweed sheet, but make sure to leave an ⅛-inch border along all four sides of the sheet uncovered. Place a quarter strip of the crab stick at the left edge of the seaweed sheet. Then begin slowly rolling from the left. When you reach the end seal the seaweed sheet together with water. Let stand about 1 minute, then using a small, very sharp knife and pressing gently to preserve the shape, cut each roll as you would a loaf of bread, making eight uniform-size sushi pieces. Repeat four more times making a total of 40 crab rolls, 6 per guest and 4 extras. The extras will allow you to weed out any pieces that are not as round or pretty as you would like.

Note: Check your local gourmet stores or organic grocery (go to the international section of the store). If that fails, try an Asian market.

Wasabi Soy Sauce Dipping Sauce

1 standard package of wet wasabi
    or 1 shaker powdered wasabi
One 10-ounce bottle of reduced sodium soy sauce

Many sushi aficionados mix wasabi with soy sauce to create a spicy dipping sauce. The amount of wasabi an individual uses is a highly personal decision. Brooksie has been known to use so much her eyes start to water when she eats the sushi. So, it's best to provide both on your table.

When serving the Slacker Sushi menu, be sure to provide each guest with either a dipping bowl or a small saucer as part of his or her place setting. Sushi lovers will automatically begin mixing the wasabi with the soy sauce in their dipping bowl. Guests trying sushi for the first time should be informed of the practice, but cautioned about the fiery nature of wasabi.

Pot Stickers

The pot stickers are even easier. For years, Morgan has kept a bag of them in her freezer, just in case guests come over. They're easy. Everyone likes them. And they hold up well in your freezer. Just heat your oven to whatever the bag says, and follow those instructions.

Two 12-ounce packages pot stickers
    (24 pieces) premade Oriental dumplings
4 tablespoons sesame oil
One 10-ounce bottle reduced-
    sodium soy sauce
Crushed red pepper
Sesame seeds

If you are still trying to fake it till you make it as a gourmet, in an Asian-style teacup, mix 1 tablespoon of the sesame oil, 1 table-spoon of the reduced-sodium soy sauce, a sprinkle of crushed red pepper and a sprinkle of sesame seeds. Now it's a dipping sauce! You will need four dipping sauce cups to adequately accommodate your guests.

Bento Box 3—Fear the Fish

If even the Slacker Sushi is too hard-core for your *rush group*, return to first principles. There is no party menu problem that cannot be fixed by putting chicken on sticks! You'll need eighteen bamboo skewers for this recipe. Just substitute chicken marinated in store-bought teriyaki sauce for the Slacker Sushi and call it Yakitori.

Yakitori

2 pounds boneless, skinless chicken breasts
1 bunch scallions, cut into ¼-inch or
**   smaller round sections**
One 10-ounce bottle commercial (store-bought)
**   teriyaki sauce**

Preheat the oven to 350 degrees. Cut the chicken into long thin strips ½-inch in width, then cut the strips into three bite-size sections. Thread the chicken sections onto bamboo skewers, inserting a scallion round in between sections. Place the skewers into a large shallow baking dish. Pour in the teriyaki sauce and marinate in the refrigerator for an hour. Bake for 20 minutes and yum! Your chicken on sticks will look as if they came from a California yakitori bar.

You might be asking, where's the white rice as a side dish? Our response: Are you mad????? Have you read the nutrition label for white rice? It's nothing but carbs, carbs, carbs. And we all know how scary that can be. We only advocate its use in sushi because it's such a small serving of rice and let's face it, sushi at home is one thing, sashimi at home is quite another.

There's also no dessert for this dinner party. In the first place, you are providing your guests with at least three courses—pot stickers, soup, and an entrée of sushi or yakitori. But fundamentally, our extensive research found that traditional and easy to prepare "Japanese" desserts appear to start and end with the frightening green tea ice cream. Not only is homemade ice cream a real pain and, therefore, a possible hazing violation, the green tea version isn't pretty and will in fact clash with your decorations. We say, dump the dessert, and just pour more sake!

Or, much like dinner at an actual sushi bar, mix and match among the bento boxes presented above to create a Bento Box 4 of your very own.

MAKE THE MOOD COME ALIVE

This should be a relaxing dinner party with a few close friends. So start by insisting that your guests remove their shoes. You may have some resistance at first, but explain they'll be more comfortable on those cushions around the coffee table without their shoes on.

Play soft instrumental music, such as a spa or tranquility CD. But counter it with anime features on the TV. What's anime? It's the politically correct term for Japanimation! Once you've had a few glasses of sake, you'll need the calm music to counter the rapid action of those cartoon cells.

Most important, serve the food on the coffee table and have your guests dine, using chopsticks of course, on the floor. Clever girl—you still have leftover chopsticks from the Chinese New Year's Party, so spread the wealth. If you're serious about home entertaining, it's always a good idea to get a bulk bag of chopsticks. So many party ideas can be made better with them!

TAKE YOUR PARTY FROM GREAT TO FIRST RATE (OR HOW WE DID IT)

Purchase a sake cup for each of your guests and using a Magic Marker for wood or a craft paint for ceramic, write their names on them (Crate & Barrel sells little wooden sake cups for 99 cents each). Personalizing the cup makes it easier to tell whom it belongs to once the sake bombs get started, and it also makes a lovely party favor.

Add another decoration to the often-overlooked party space that is your bathroom. Float candles and fresh cherry blossoms in an inch of water in your bathtub.

Rent or borrow a karaoke machine. Party Math: Sake + karaoke = people laughing so hard they fall off their cushions—which are conveniently on the floor.

TIMELINE

In Washington, D.C., events associated with the National Cherry Blossom Festival start around the end of March and continue through the middle of April. Depending on the weather, the blossoms peak during the first week of April. If your community holds Cherry Blossom Festival events, we suggest you time your party to coincide, but not conflict, with a popular event such as the parade, by hosting your dinner party that evening. If your dinner party will be the *only* Cherry Blossom Festival event for your community, select a date in the first or second week of April to host your event.

Let's talk about guest lists. There's an "A list" and there's a "B list." Your "A list" people are the first choice for the elite six cushions around your coffee table. Start your oral invitations with the "A list," realizing that people may have family obligations, prior commitments, or evil work responsibilities that preclude their ability to accept such an exclusive invitation. But, with that said, remember that personalities count. For example although Bob is a great conversationalist and has fantastic green eyes, you may choose to promote plainer Bill if Bob is not the kind of guy who will remove his shoes and play along.

Two weeks before the dinner—Call and invite your guests. It's a short invite list, so spend a little a time on the phone telling them how much fun this will be.

Ten days before the dinner—Select your bento box menu. Should you opt for Bento Box 1, call and place the order for your sushi.

One week before the dinner—Inventory the decorations you plan to recycle and check to see if you need to fill in any holes. Purchase cherry blossom garlands. Gather the items needed for your Shinto shrine centerpiece. Order your flower arrangements.

The evening before the dinner—Tidy up your party space. Should you choose Bento Box 2 or Bento Box 3 make your trip to the grocery store.

The morning of the dinner—Pedicure—remember, you won't be wearing any shoes either so make sure your feet look nice and smell pretty. Purchase the sake and pick up the flowers. Rent anime movies. Assemble the Shinto shrine centerpiece.

The afternoon of the dinner—Enjoy your community's Cherry Blossom parade, if applicable.

5 P.M.	Bento Box 2 partyers: Begin to boil the water for the sushi rice. Bento Box 3 partyers: Cut the chicken, thread the chicken and scallions onto the sticks, and marinate the chicken sticks in teriyaki sauce.
5:15 P.M.	Bento Box 2 partyers: While the rice cooks, make the rice wine vinegar, ginger, and sugar, mixture.
5:40 P.M.	Bento Box 2 partyers: Remove the cooked rice from the heat and drain and place in a non-metallic shallow dish, starting the separation process as previously described.
6 P.M.	Bento Box 1 partyers: Pick up the sushi.
6:30 P.M.	Hang lanterns, place flowers, hang garlands, and place centerpiece.
6:45 P.M.	Bento Box 2 partyers: Shape one quarter of the sushi rice into twelve 1-inch-long bundles, reserve the rest to be spread over the seaweed wraps.

7 P.M.	Freshen your makeup and check your hair. Bento Box 3 partyers: Put the chicken in the oven.
7:15 P.M.	Pop dumplings into the oven, begin to heat the Miso Soup mix. If you've selected Bento Box 2, Slacker Sushi, form sushi as described in recipe.
7:30 P.M.	Greet your guests and insist everyone remove their shoes, scowling at those who refuse until they comply.

A WORD ABOUT . . . JAPANESE CUISINE BASICS

Think back to your SAT days and enjoy this analogy word puzzle:

> As Americans are to happy meals,
> The Japanese are to bento boxes.

So think of this as your SSBs: sake, sushi, and bento boxes. While millions of Americans purchase the traditionally black and lacquered compartmentalized food trays and think of them as a kind of art, in Japanese cuisine, the bento box is synonymous with fast food. Our

friend Lil' Jimmy reports that in Japan you can buy them at 7-Eleven and gas stations and surprisingly the sushi is still good.

In general the bento box is designed to maximize simplicity and artful presentation by compartmentalizing the food, making it easy to serve and eat, and at the same time allowing a variety of flavors to be presented together.

A bento box involves different flavors and textures, which can include a sushi portion. Not too long ago, before sushi was available in grocery stores from Wyoming to Ohio, before you could find good sushi restaurants in landlocked cities like Tulsa (seriously, go to "In the Raw" in Brookside), eating sushi was a sign of bravery and adventurism. Today, eating sushi is a great way to manage your diet while having a meal out.

In Japan, sushi is a popular food that can even be found served on conveyor belts self-serve style in certain bargain restaurants. Sushi generally refers to a dish containing rice that has been treated with sushi vinegar. Sushi with seafood, especially uncooked seafood, is the most well-known application. However, as the above recipes show, sushi doesn't have to include the much-maligned "raw fish" preparation, sometimes derisively referred to as "bait" by some of our less cultured relatives. In addition, sushi can be vegetarian, can be served with or without dried seaweed wraps, or, in the case of Inari, is deep-fried. If you are experiencing sushi for the first time, start slow. Know your limits. If you've never eaten eel before and you don't like trying new food, perhaps you should start with some California rolls. Sushi represents a nearly endless variety of combinations; you're bound to find something you like. Or, if all else fails, order the teriyaki and just concentrate on mastering your appreciation of sake.

EASTER BRUNCH

Because brunch is way easier than dinner,

and you get your family out of your house faster.

CONCEPT

Let's face it, sooner or later familial obligations catch up with all of us. But just because your parents are coming over doesn't mean you have to tube the entire day. Herein lies the beauty of a meal called brunch. Not quite breakfast and not quite lunch, plus if you host it before the family goes to church on Easter Sunday, you've got the clock ticking.

A little proactive defense can get you out of a lot of work and allow you to retain your reputation as the perfect child. Instead of avoiding the division of labor that are family get-togethers, volunteer early—for Easter. If you don't, you'll find everyone looking at you kind of funny until you hear an overly cheerful voice that kind of sounds like yours volunteering to host everyone for Thanksgiving. Besides, if you plan it right, you can have everyone in and out in less than 2 hours. Can we get an Amen?

It's Easter, so your colors are pale pink—think Japanese cherry blossom—pale yellow, and pale green. Since it's brunch, and you are probably coming from or going to Easter services, no one expects you to have a lot of deco-

DECORATIONS

One 6-foot strand of cherry blossom
garland—recycled from the Japanese
Cherry Blossom Festival
1 vase
Nice china and table linens or heavy-duty
plates and nice paper products

rations. Focus on your table centerpiece by wrapping your cherry blossom garland around the inside of a clear vase.

Your faithful founders recognize that Easter is a family holiday and most people already have specific traditions. No matter how stupid, outdated, or goofy you think these family traditions might be, you have to incorporate them into your brunch, because if you don't, it's guaranteed to start an argument.[2]

If you have nice china and table linens, go

ahead and use them. If you don't own nice china, buy some pale pink or yellow paper napkins, but splurge on the nicer, heavy-duty dinner plate—think "Chinette."

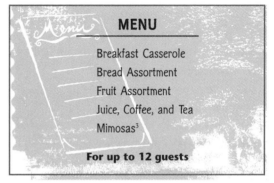

MENU

Breakfast Casserole

Bread Assortment

Fruit Assortment

Juice, Coffee, and Tea

Mimosas[3]

For up to 12 guests

Breakfast Casserole

The Breakfast Casserole must be made the night before in order to set and cook properly. To make twelve servings, you will need two 2-quart square baking dishes (disposable foil dishes can be used if you don't already own the baking dishes). We'll do the math so you can make them one at a time with ease.

---

2. Drunken arguments with friends are considered lively conversations. Arguments with family members at social events are fodder for long-term resentment and the need for family therapy.

3. If your family does not drink, but you do, just make a screwdriver. Vodka has no smell, so everyone will think the first two are just orange juice.

Fat-free cooking spray

8 English muffins

One 10-ounce package frozen broccoli,
thawed and drained

2 cups cubed cooked ham

One 12-ounce package fat-free
Cheddar cheese, shredded

2 cups egg substitute

3 ½ cups fat-free milk

1 cup fat-free sour cream

2 teaspoons onion powder

2 teaspoons pepper

2 tablespoons Dijon mustard

Start by spraying the 2-quart square baking dish with the fat-free cooking spray. Next, tear two English muffins into bite-size pieces and cover the bottom of the dish with the torn muffin chunks. Layer 5 ounces of the broccoli, 1 cup of the cubed ham, and 6 ounces of the fat-free Cheddar cheese on top of the torn English muffin pieces. Take another two English muffins and tear them into bite-size pieces to top the casserole.

In a mixing bowl, combine ½ cup of the egg substitute, 1¾ cups of the fat-free milk, ½ cup of the fat-free sour cream, 1 teaspoon of the onion powder, 1 teaspoon of the pepper, and 1 tablespoon of the Dijon mustard. Whisk until smooth. Pour this mixture over the casserole; cover and refrigerate overnight.

Since you've only just made six servings, you'll need to repeat the above process in your second 2-quart square baking pan. In the morning, you'll bake these casseroles in a preheated 350 degree oven for 50 to 55 minutes.

Bread Assortment

6 croissants

6 rolls

6 muffins

While doing your grocery shopping for this event, purchase a nice array of breakfast breads. We suggest 6 croissants, 6 rolls, and 6 muffins. Try to keep them sealed tightly or stash them in the microwave until 15 minutes before your family arrives. Place a pastel-colored dish or hand towel in the bottom of a lovely serving basket or your Easter basket from last year. Then put the assorted breads in the basket and wrap the towel around the bread. Place on the food table.

Mimosas

1 gallon reduced-carb and calcium-enriched
orange juice

2 bottles of Italian Prosecco

1 small bottle grenadine

We always tell you, don't try to fight tradition. Traditions are part of what makes special events memorable. With that in mind, there are two cocktails that are inextricably linked to brunch culture. Of course we are speaking of the bloody mary and the mimosa. In this case we are counseling you to go mimosa. First off, many people find tomato juice scary and it may negatively impact the health of your carpet. Second, mimosas are made with champagne or a sparkling white wine and anytime that you can justifiably open your first bottle of white before noon, that is a *great* Rho Sigma Gamma day!

But maybe your family doesn't share those views, or is Pentecostal, so for that reason we have provided below three possible Mimosa recipes in various speeds: (1) Pentecostal (virgin); (2) Restaurant style (a moderate approach reminiscent of a restaurant brunch—in other words not too much wine); and (3) "My Family's So Dysfunctional, Get Me the Wine So I Won't Notice the Bloodshed." Aka #3.

In general, mimosas are not at their best served punch-bowl style, so plan to make them individually and serve them in champagne flutes. Time is tight, so procure supplies for no more than two drinks per likely drinker. For restaurant style, anticipate six mimosas per standard (750-ml) bottle of sparkling white. Reduce that calculation to four if you are serving #3. The traditional, or restaurant-style, mimosa is a blend of orange juice and champagne. In general, you should fill a champagne flute with equal parts orange juice and champagne. However, you are not an "in-general" type of girl! Spice things up a bit. Never use plain orange juice when a calcium-enriched or reduced-carb option is available. Also, Italian Prosecco sparkling white is a touch sweeter than regular champagne. It's a great counterpoint to your nutritionally altered juice. Then, serve the drinks "sunrise style" with a splash of grenadine. Sunrise service meet sunrise cocktail!

For Pentecostal mimosas substitute a sparkling grape juice for the Prosecco. And for #3, fill the flute with Prosecco, add a splash of juice, and then a splash of grenadine. Drink quickly and pray that your family will go away. It's yet another Easter blessing.

Fruit Assortment

1 cantaloupe
1 honeydew melon
1 pint strawberries

Don't worry, your tour of kitchen duty is nearly over. All that's left is a little melon baller time and cleaning those strawberries. Once your fruit is cut (unless you were a smart girl and bought the precut fruit platter in the produce section), you're done! Just keep it in the fridge overnight.

MAKE THE MOOD COME ALIVE

Easter isn't really about a mood or an atmosphere. This party is your opportunity to be a part of your family's holiday schedule. And because you've chosen to host brunch, you're probably responsible for getting everyone to church on time. Besides, after church, you get to go home, take a nap, and let your mom or sister worry about cooking that big Easter dinner.

TAKE YOUR PARTY FROM GREAT TO FIRST RATE (OR HOW WE DID IT)

Add the traditional decoration of dyed Easter eggs. Dye a dozen Easter eggs in pale pink, yellow, and green and place them in small bowls on the table, in the bathroom, or in other spots where people might gather.

Kiss up to your family. Buy your older female relatives Easter corsages. Participate in your church's Easter flower donation program and purchase a lily in honor of your family.

Reward everyone for leaving on time for church with a party favor. Purchase two large bags of jelly beans and enough plastic eggs for each of your guests. Fill half the egg with jelly beans and distribute the eggs as your guests leave.

TIMELINE

Good Friday (if you have the day off) or the Saturday before Easter—Go to the grocery store.

Saturday evening—Make the breakfast casseroles, cut and clean the fruit, prepare the centerpiece, and set the table. Taking care of everything tonight means you can sleep longer tomorrow! And there is no beauty treatment better than adequate rest.

Sunday—1 hour before the family arrives, put the Breakfast Casserole in the oven and get ready while it bakes.

30 minutes before they arrive—Mix your first mimosa.

15 minutes before your family arrives—Put the fruit and bread assortment out on the table. Make first pot of coffee. Set out tea and juice.

A WORD ABOUT . . . AVOIDING FAMILY FIGHTS

Let's face it, family get-togethers are stressful. While we realize that no Recovering Sorority Girl would ever be the cause of familial strife, we do recognize that it is easy to get caught up in it. Again, we suggest you host brunch before going to church. While everyone may have to get up a little earlier, they might be too tired to fight. Plus, you have a definite party-ending time—when you have to leave for church.

With the clock ticking, most people will just be concerned about eating. If your mom starts in about what you are wearing, or your dad asks why they haven't promoted you, respond with an Easter-themed question such as, "What do you think Reverend So-and-So will discuss today?" Or if you want to go for the jugular, try this response, "Mom, the Lord has risen, let's not fight over something silly. Would you like more coffee?" Trust us—she'll step back faster than the reigning international ballroom dance champion.

As a rule of thumb, avoid topics that will set your family off—and stop pretending you don't know what we are talking about, because we know you do! Just keep thinking about the fact that you are going to church and by hosting Easter Brunch you don't have to invite them over for another year. And if this fails, we recommend that you pour a good stiff drink into your coffee cup and see if anyone notices. Besides, they'll be giving you wine at church, so you're already planning to drink before noon.

MORGAN'S TOP TEN PARTY ESSENTIALS

1. Blender

    Margaritas to crepes to clever purees, a blender can do it all. More cost-effective than a food processor and a lot less complex.

2. A series of decorative bowls

    A series of bowls in various sizes that are dishwasher safe and complement your home's decor can greatly uncomplicate food presentation and unify your party look with your home's style.

3. Decorative linens

    Personally, I'm a sucker for the Pottery Barn sale table. Sure you buy out of season, but nothing compares to the thrill of finding an $80 silver organza snowflake tablecloth for $27.

4. Condiment serving piece

    Either a series of small bowls or trays that can accent your food area and unify your condiment presentation with the rest of your festive food display. My favorite piece is a wrought-iron ring with three smaller attached rings that hold 3 glass bowls. A great way to serve chips and a variety of salsas or a deli tray with a selection of spicy mustards and mayonnaise.

5. Tiffany ice bucket

    If there are beverages, there will be a need for ice, so why not serve it from a Tiffany bucket?

6. A series of crystal candlesticks

    Tiffany, if you have them, to go with the ice bucket. Or also add a series of inexpensive ones so that you can make a more dramatic display.

7. An electric knife

    Under no circumstances should you attempt hors d'oeuvres without one. Easy crostini. Finely sliced roast beef.

8. A large collection of inexpensive glassware

    Sometimes, your drinks just won't taste right in plastic. If it's not going to taste right, don't serve it!

9. 1 large, attractive basket

    An ideal way to present silverware, bread, cloth napkins, party favors, or anything that you can name. A must-have.

10. A fondue pot

    Inexpensive, versatile, good for hors d'oeuvres, desserts, and a great conversational activity.

BROOKSIE'S TOP TEN PARTY ESSENTIALS

1. Paper towels
    Spills happen. Don't be anal. Just have enough paper towels to clean up.

2. Carpet cleaner
    See #1. One bottle of spray carpet pretreater.

3. An elegantly set table
    You don't need fine china to create an interesting and inviting food table—although it helps. Think multidimensional. Use martini glasses to hold dips, baskets for bread or chips, and coffee cups to hold utensils. Turn some bowls upside down to create a riser for a casserole. Whether you purchased everything from a deli or prepared it all from scratch, an elegantly set table will earn you compliments.

4. Toilet paper
    Sadly, yes I do have to write it on my list. In order to protect the innocent, I won't name names, but you know who you are and you need to buy some toilet paper before you invite people over again!

5. A wine bottle opener you can actually operate
    For a year, I had the worst bottle opener ever designed and was forced to rely on the wine-opening skills of my pretend boyfriend or risk being forced to strain my wine through a sieve. Spend the money and make sure you can operate it.

6. **Some basic knowledge about your guests**

   Have you ever attended a party where you only knew the hostess and she didn't introduce you to anyone? It probably sucked. Practice your *bumping* and *rotating* skills so you can introduce people who have common interests.

7. **The number of a local cab company**

   I love to party. I enjoy my white wine. I realize that many of my guests are the same way. However, as a hostess I also have the responsibility of making sure my guests get home safely. In my community, calling a cab is not an odd thing to do. So when your guests are having lots of fun, be sure to have a *risk management* plan to keep them safe.

8. **A menu that matches the time of your party**

   If your party starts between 5 P.M. and 8 P.M., your guests haven't eaten dinner and will be expecting something substantial such as heavy hors d'ouevres or a solid casserole. After 9 P.M., you can get away with lighter fare.

9. **A solid RSVP list**

   It's difficult to do your shopping without it!

10. **Helpers**

    No, I'm not referring to the staff I have in my imagination. At every party, I task a girlfriend or two to help with little items like making sure we have continuous music and ensuring the food table never looks too bare. No one has ever refused my request for assistance, so either they truly do not mind or they are too afraid to tell me.

Chapter Five

MAY

ARE YOU A DERBY PERSON OR A CINCO DE MAYO PERSON?

A RANT BY MORGAN

Sometimes, the party gods are inexplicably cruel in their plenty and provide too many celebrations too close together on the calendar. The result for a dedicated hostess or a faithful *sister* of RSG is that not every celebration may be appropriately marked. Although the Thanksgiving-Christmas-New Year's juggernaut is an example of this cruel overscheduling, the tightest timeline by far is the Kentucky Derby–Cinco de Mayo period.

You see, outside of Mexico, Cinco de Mayo parties are typically held the weekend nearest to the Fifth of May itself. This means that your party will fall on the first or second weekend in May. Horse-racing tradition states that the Kentucky Derby will be raced on the first Saturday in May. What is a Recovering Sorority Girl to do? Combine party themes should the parties fall on the same day? Never! Theme articulation is crucial to a unique home-entertaining experience. Mixed themes are the party equivalent of a rummage sale, full of stuff that doesn't quite match.

Then, are you expected to throw two parties one week apart? That also is a bit extreme. There are times in life when hard choices must be made. This is one of those times. We suggest the following solution: If you are a Derby person, we recommend that you host a derby party and then convert the Cinco de Mayo model provided in these pages to a Mexican Fiesta that can be put together for Memorial Day weekend. If you are a Cinco de Mayo person, we invite you to adapt the Kentucky Derby party to a Preakness Stakes Party or a Belmont Stakes Party. If you have to choose between the two, we recommend that you select the Preakness, because New York just doesn't have the same type of evocative cuisine as Kentucky and Maryland. Substitute mini-broiled crab cakes for the Faux Fried Chicken and Black-Eyed Susan Punch for the Mint Juleps and voilà: instant Maryland cool. If you take the option of the Preakness Party, please consult www.recoveringsororitygirls.com for those recipes.

So, how do you know if you are a Derby person or a Cinco de Mayo person? Well, we have thoughtfully provided this highly unscientific quiz. Just select your preferences between two items:

1. Barn dog or Chihuahua?
2. Bourbon or tequila?
3. Mint or lime?
4. Nicely trimmed straw hat or sombrero?
5. Horse or burro?
6. Picnic or burrito bar?
7. Bluegrass or Latin pop?
8. Miller or Corona?
9. Nascar or Telemundo?

If you prefer more of the first items, then you are a Derby person. If you prefer more of the second, then you are a Cinco de Mayo person. Plan to party accordingly.

KENTUCKY DERBY

And they're off!

CONCEPT

Although horse racing is called the Sport of Kings for most of the year, only old white men in bad polyester jackets, aka compulsive gamblers, find it interesting. But during May and the first part of June, all kinds of people engage in a ritual event known as the Triple Crown. The jewel of the crown is the Kentucky Derby. The derby started in 1875, around the time that collegiate Greek life was founded in America. The derby continues to be run at Churchill Downs, a grand old Southern race park. Today, when most people think about the derby they think of the rollicking crowds of the infield, ladies in fine hats up in the stands, and many Mint Juleps for all. Similar attachments are formed for the other two jewels in the crown: Maryland's Preakness Stakes at Pimlico (Baltimore) and New York's Belmont Stakes (Long Island).

Chances are you and your friends are racing novices and can't tell Bob Baffert from the mayor of Louisville. We sure can't. But just because you are unaware of the hottest horse trainers or the winning records of the various jockeys doesn't mean you should be deprived of

DECORATIONS

Red-and-white-checked vinyl tablecloth—
    size and shape to cover your food table
18 plastic or paper plates, assorted colors
24 napkins, assorted colors
18 sets of plastic cutlery
24 clear plastic cups, assorted colors
1 small red or white horseshoe-shaped
    flower arrangement
1 large picnic basket
1 punch bowl (sized to fit inside the empty
    picnic basket)
1 package of construction paper—various
    colors, including black
1 craft glue stick
2 thumbtacks
1 string (to go the length of one wall of
    your party space)
Clothespins
Ice packs
Festive cloth or dish towels
Scissors
Plain paper
Black Magic Marker
1 roll of wall-safe tape

your derby fun. All celebrations break out to three key elements: shared activity, a good food/drink menu, and the right combination of people. Whether or not you can name all of the horses prior to post time, you can still maximize the three essential party elements for an afternoon everyone will remember.

A red-and-white-checked tablecloth will make its debut at this party. You know the one, you've seen it in pictures of picnics and at Italian restaurants all of your life. If you can't find one already made, major fabric stores sell this particular vinyl on 54-inch-wide rolls for a little more than $5.00 a yard. Measure your table and head on over to get yourself a kitschy but effective table covering. The decorations on the food table will be rounded out with your coordinating plates, napkins, cutlery, and cups, a small, white or red horseshoe flower arrangement as the centerpiece, and a large picnic basket, which will be placed at the end of your food table closest to your party space.

Open the picnic basket and place your punch bowl inside. You will be using the punch bowl to serve and store your juleps. Keep your julep punch cold by wrapping ice packs in festive cloth or dish towels and packing the ice packs around the sides of the punch bowl in the gaps between the basket and the bowl. What a clever girl you are! No one will see the ice, and nothing will water down the bourbon. Near brilliant!

Finally, you'll also be making racing silks out of construction paper. Examples of racing silk patterns can be found on the Internet and in most cases are easy to duplicate using only two or three colors and simple geometric shapes. Use one sheet of construction paper as your base and cut the shapes for the silks out of another color. Glue-stick the color shapes onto the base. Make enough silks to create a nice banner that will run the length of your party space. Use the thumbtacks to secure the string to the wall and hang the racing silks from the string with the clothespins. Also make silks for your refrigerator door and the interior doors of the party-accessible bathroom(s). Tape them to those spaces.

However, this party really isn't about decorations; it's about preparing to watch and then seeing the derby on television. Don't be afraid to move your TV into the middle of the party space, Super Bowl–style.

Faux Fried Chicken

Real fried chicken, though traditional and tasty, is not an option given that bathing suit season will descend three short weeks after the derby. Much like a faux tan protects against cancer, Faux Fried Chicken protects against the horror of cellulite. Keep the taste, but lose the fat and go faux.

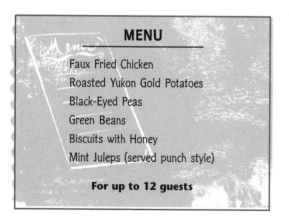

1 ¾ cups yellow cornmeal
1 ¼ cups flour
Dash of salt
1 ¾ teaspoons black pepper
40 chicken legs, bought skinless or skin removed
4 egg whites
3 ½ teaspoons paprika (see Note for more
   information)

Preheat the oven to 375 degrees. Combine the cornmeal, flour, salt, pepper, and paprika in a Ziploc bag. Roll the chicken legs in the egg whites and then shake in a plastic bag until coated. Place a leg on an aluminum-foil-covered baking sheet that has been sprayed with

---

MENU

Faux Fried Chicken
Roasted Yukon Gold Potatoes
Black-Eyed Peas
Green Beans
Biscuits with Honey
Mint Juleps (served punch style)

For up to 12 guests

cooking spray. Once all of the legs have been placed on sheets, spray each leg with cooking spray briefly to moisten. Bake for forty minutes until chicken is tender.

Note: If you like spicier foods, use 1³/₄ teaspoons cayenne pepper instead of the paprika.

Roasted Yukon Gold Potatoes

The roasted potatoes can be baked concurrently with the chicken on the upper shelf of your oven.

Fat-free cooking spray
3 teaspoons olive oil
3 teaspoons Old Bay seasoning
3 teaspoons paprika
3 teaspoons dry mustard
3 teaspoons black pepper
3 teaspoons dried parsley
Dash of salt
Red pepper
7 pounds Yukon gold potatoes (approximately
    10 medium-size potatoes), peeled and cut
    into ¹/₄-inch cubes

Preheat the oven to 375 degrees. Spray an aluminum-foil-covered sheet cake pan with the cooking spray. Add a layer of 1 teaspoon of the olive oil, Old Bay seasoning, paprika, dry mus-

tard, black pepper, and parsley as well as a dash of salt to the pan, then add half the potatoes. Repeat the process, adding another layer of seasonings and another layer of potatoes. Mix the layers, and add the final layer of seasonings and then mix again. Bake on the top shelf of your oven for fifty minutes until the potatoes are tender and golden.

Black-Eyed Peas and Green Beans

Three 15-ounce cans black-eyed peas, drained
Three 16-ounce bags frozen French-cut
    green beans
3 teaspoons white vinegar
4 slices cooked bacon, crumbled
2 teaspoons chopped scallions

The black-eyed peas and green beans should be gently warmed over low heat in separate pots. To the black-eyed peas add the crumbled bacon and chopped scallions. To the green beans add the white vinegar to give the beans "Southern" flavor.

Biscuits

Four 12-ounce packages ready-to-bake biscuits
One 12-ounce honey bear of honey
1 small decorative plate arranged with
    pats of stick margarine in a circular
    pattern with butter serving fork

As for the biscuits, they come out of a tube, you do the math. Hey, you've already made the chicken and the potatoes from scratch! Who are you? Betty Crocker? Just follow the instructions on the side of the tube.

Mint Juleps

O.K., no one under fifty who doesn't bear more than a passing resemblance to Colonel Sanders actually *likes* bourbon. It burns! It's thick, and Morgan is still recovering from the memory of a week-long bourbon hangover incurred during the summer before her senior year of college. But tradition is tradition and adherence to tradition is a valuable part of establishing theme, especially when your theme is built around an already well-known event. So, bourbon it is.

Since we anticipate that your guests will have misgivings about bourbon too, we suggest that you serve it punch style! We have added water and Splenda simple syrup to disrupt the bourbon burn and to help your guests remain largely hangover-free. Why Splenda simple syrup? Straight bourbon and mint is obviously out of the question. If your body is going to endure the hardship of bourbon there is no need to add the calories of actual sugar to the mix. Tradition is important, but let's not lose sight of our priorities.

8 cups Splenda

3 quarts very cold water plus 2 quarts water (for simple syrup)

Three ¾-ounce packages fresh mint leaves

3 liters (two 1.5-liter bottles) fine Kentucky bourbon

Start by making your Splenda simple syrup. In a large saucepan, mix the Splenda with equal parts of water (aka 2 quarts). Stir the water-Splenda mixture over low heat until the Splenda is mostly dissolved. Stop stirring at this point or else you will disrupt the syrup. Raise the heat to medium and simmer for 3 minutes. Remove from the heat and let the syrup cool.

Remove the mint from the packages. Wash the mint thoroughly in a colander and pull the leaves off the stems. Bruise the mint or put it in a blender or food processor on pulse, and chop it into large pieces.

Add 1.5 liters of bourbon to a large punch bowl. To minimize that bourbon burn, freeze it overnight. Trust us, you'll thank us for this later, especially during those first two mint juleps. Add 1½ quarts of the very cold water to the punch bowl. Next add half the Splenda simple syrup. Finally add half the mint pieces. Stir. After the first punch bowl has been drained, repeat the punch mixture as described above.

To serve, use small clear plastic cocktail cups. Keep the portions small. Seriously, and we will never say this about an alcoholic beverage again—3 ounces. Your guests and your carpet will thank you later.

MAKE THE MOOD COME ALIVE

Since the decorations are sparse, it's important to truly set the mood for this party. You'll have the derby pregame show on the television, but it's important to keep your guests focused on the general theme. So, we suggest you open the betting booth. The better you are at math, the more complex you can make it by adding odds and all kinds of bets. But since Brooksie barely made it through statistics with a C and Morgan didn't fare much better, we've kept our betting booth pretty simple.

Make horse cutouts by either purchasing dye cuts at the local craft store or photocopying the outline of a horse onto plain paper and making a stencil that can be used to trace the horse outline onto black construction paper. Make as many horses as you have guests. Arrange the horses, a list of the horses running in the race, and a black Magic Marker in your party entry area. Have each of your guests

write the name of the horse they are betting on and his or her own name on "their" horse.

The winner gets to take the small, horseshoe-shaped flower arrangement home. In the event of a tie, the guest who selected the winning horse first is the winner, thereby encouraging party punctuality.

TAKE YOUR PARTY FROM GREAT TO FIRST RATE (OR HOW WE DID IT)

Atmosphere, atmosphere, atmosphere. Demand that your guests wear their Derby bests—seersucker suits for the men and sundresses and hats for the ladies. This creates instant Southern sorority girl charm! Encourage a little Southern eccentricity and offer fabulous prizes for the biggest, gaudiest hats.

Use galvanized steel tubs for both form and function. They make a fabulous decoration and can be used to hold beer, soft drinks, and ice for those guests who are intimidated by the Mint Juleps.

Explore a music genre you are probably not familiar with—bluegrass. Be sure to have plenty of music for after the derby. Just because the Derby is over by late afternoon does not mean your party should stop. If your guests have shown up in true Derby finery, take your show on the road to a bluegrass club in your community.

TIMELINE

Two weeks before the Derby—Send out your e-mail invitation and start shopping for your hat. Remember to select one that will complement your dress *and* your hairstyle. Buy decorations and supplies and procure music.

    One week before the party—Start making the silks, a few each day. Order the floral arrangement. Have your spring/summer hair color applied by a professional. RSG members do *not* use color from a box.

    The night before the party—Go to the grocery store. Purchase and freeze bourbon.

    The morning of the party—Pick up the flower arrangement.

2:30 P.M.	Cook the bacon until crisp and then set it aside in refrigerator.
2:35 P.M.	Chop potatoes, place in baking pan.
3 P.M.	Coat the chicken with the flour mixture, place on foil-lined baking sheets. Spice the potatoes.

3:15 P.M.	The chicken and potatoes are put into the oven.
3:30 P.M.	Hair and makeup final touches.
3:55 P.M.	Heat the black-eyed peas and green beans on low. Remove the chicken from the oven.
4 P.M.	Hang the silks; arrange the betting booth.
4:15 P.M.	Remove the potatoes from the oven. Put the biscuits on a baking sheet and into the oven. Make the simple syrup. Assemble the punch bowl.
4:30 P.M.	Guests arrive, begin to mix Mint Juleps. Open the betting booth.

A WORD ABOUT . . . SIMPLE SYRUP

Our extensive research has demonstrated that most people don't like the taste of hard liquor. Even Morgan and Brooksie are not known to drink the stuff straight—well, not unless it's near the end of the evening, it's served in shots, and a dare is involved. A good drink is one that has achieved a balance between the rough edges of the liquor and the smoothing effects of the mixer or dilution.

In general, there are three ways to make a cocktail sweeter to balance the bitterness of the liquor: add juice, add straight sugar, or use simple syrup. Clearly, of the three, simple syrup is the most difficult. But for many drinks it is frankly the most tasty. Look, we try to keep your lives easy; we know that you have a lot of things keeping you busy. But sometimes to make your guests comfortable and to make the drink worth drinking, you have to suffer for your art. So, several times a year, show your guests how special they are and bust out the simple syrup. Believe us, everyone will appreciate it.

CINCO DE MAYO

Two shakers of salt . . .

CONCEPT

Have we said tequila yet? You don't have to be Mexican to be glad Mexico is free! Think of how their advancements in all-inclusive resorts and swim-up bar technology might have been delayed had Mexico not achieved independence. Cinco de Mayo marks the victory of the Mexican Army over the French at the Battle of Puebla, demonstrating to the world that Mexico and all of Latin America were willing to defend themselves against foreign intervention. In addition to yet another great opportunity to cel-

ebrate the defeat of the personal hygiene–challenged French, Cinco de Mayo is a great party!

This party invites you to step into a Jose Cuervo ad campaign and shake your bonbon to some great MTV en Español tunes. Much like St. Patrick's Day when everyone is Irish, on Cinco de Mayo, everyone in North America truly is Mexican. Even you Texans—come on, admit it!

Some of you may have acquired a fear of tequila through a spring break incident, your twenty-first birthday party, or some other similar event. Now is the time for you to face this fear. We would never, ever hurt you. So trust us, and turn up the Telemundo.

DECORATIONS

30 paper or plastic plates in red, green, or white

40 napkins in red, green, or white

30 sets of plastic cutlery

40 plastic cups in red, green, or white

3 small piñatas

Your old Mexican blanket

8 hand-painted Mexican tiles (check the local Dollar Store)

3 strands of 100 white Christmas tree lights per 1,500 square feet of party space

10 small silver gift bags

Three 1-pound bags of craft sand

2 soccer schedules

10 plain votive holders, shatterproof glass or plastic preferred

10 plain white votive candles

Several empty tequila bottles of varying size

Tin-punch stencil

Small utility knife

1 hole punch (or several scrapbooking hole punches in various shapes)

Just a few simple decorations, a great burrito bar, and of course, our good friend, tequila, make this party more tempting than a weekend in Puerto Vallarta. Besides tipsy adults whacking the hell out of a papier-mâché bull is either really funny or a story that ends with the phrase, "and then we went to the emergency room."

Take your colors from the flag of Mexico—red, green, and white. This creates an opportunity to recycle from your previous parties. So if you have a few red plates left over from Valentine's Day and some green plates left over from St. Patrick's Day, don't be afraid to mix and match. If you restack the plates and alternate the colors—your *rush group* will think you did it on purpose.

Find some small piñatas at the discount party store to decorate your party space and food table. Be sure to pick colors that complement your decor. Use one for your food table, and then hang the other two in an area that is conducive to blindfolded drunk people swinging sticks. If you have a patio or deck, it may be a better option for the second two.

Dining is very important in Mexican culture. Most anthropologists attribute this characteristic to the Aztec and Spanish influences. The ancient Aztecs thought man had come from corn and this belief led to various dining rules that divided the social classes. The Spanish imported elaborate food traditions of their own as well as strict rules associated with the Catholic calendar of holy days. Modern Mexico still retains many of these influences. Even today, daily life revolves around the midday meal or *comida*, which is usually from 2 P.M. to 4 P.M. More than any other meal, *comida* is still structured as it was 100 years ago and is as much a social affair as it is a meal. To carry forth this rich cultural tradition, you'll want to pay special attention to your food table, making it a centerpiece in and of itself.

Instead of using a tablecloth, use your Mexican blanket to cover the food table. Because you are creating a burrito bar, you will need to have varying degrees of height on your food table. You may want to stand some mixing bowls upside down on your uncovered table first to create little stands for condiments. For your hot dishes, use your hand-painted Mexican tiles as trivets.

If you have an outdoor party space, now is the time to start using it. Just make sure you provide ample outdoor seating because if the weather is starting to warm up, people will probably want to be outside.

String those white Christmas tree lights along your porch railing if you have one. Otherwise loop the lights throughout your party space or perhaps use a ladder and thumbtacks

to attach them to the ceiling of your main party room. Now, it's time to make the silver luminarias. Again, the Internet is your best friend. Search for a standard punched-tin pattern and then print it out to use as a stencil. Cut out the outline of your stencil with a small, narrow utility knife. Place the cutout over each silver gift bag and then repeat the process with the utility knife. Make sure your stencil is not too large or too deep as you will need to leave enough solid bag to retain a level of sand deep enough to hold the luminaria's votive candle in place. Once the stenciling is complete, add the sand, place the candle inside, and repeat with the remaining bags.

With the sand that's left, fill those empty tequila bottles and set them out on end tables, coffee tables, etc. It'll add a hint of cheesy tourist trap and remind your guests that tequila truly is the national drink of Mexico, so a margarita or four won't hurt them.

And we can't forget the bathrooms. Tape one of your soccer schedules up on the bathroom doors and the other directly across from the toilet. Hey, just because people have to use the rest room doesn't mean they can escape from your party theme.

MENU

Burrito Bar
Chips and Dips (Guacamole and Salsa)
Tequila Lime Mousse
Margaritas

For up to 20 guests

Burrito Bar

No, it isn't a typo when we tell you to buy eighty corn tortillas. Yes, it sounds like a lot, but it's only four per guest, and they are pretty small. Besides, once your guests try their first shrimp burrito, they'll be back for at least seconds.

Any fool can tell you to go the store and buy Old El Paso Taco mix or a fajita kit. However, we think that you are better than that, so we have provided you with a menu that presents certain Mexican-American cuisine flavors, but at the same time is unique and yummy.

3 pounds peeled, deveined shrimp
   (fresh or fresh frozen, but not frozen)
¼ cup white cooking wine
   (use 1 tablespoon at a time)
¼ cup Rose's Lime Juice
   (use 1 tablespoon at a time)
2 tablespoons chili powder

2 small dried habanero chili peppers
5 pounds boneless, skinless chicken breasts,
   cut into ¼-inch cubes
Two 15-ounce cans fat-free vegetarian
   refried beans
Two 15-ounce cans black beans
2 green bell peppers
2 medium-size red onions
4 cups white rice
Eighty 4½-inch corn tortillas
16 ounces shredded Monterey Jack cheese
One 16-ounce container fat-free sour cream

Start by grabbing your trusty nonstick skillet to sauté the shrimp. Ideally, your skillet is large enough to accommodate all the shrimp, 2 tablespoons of the cooking wine, 2 tablespoons of the lime juice, 1 tablespoon of the chili powder, and 1 dried habanero pepper at one time. If not, sauté in two equal batches of 1 tablespoon white cooking wine, 1 tablespoon Rose's Lime Juice, 2 teaspoons chili powder, and one half dried habanera pepper. Cook until the shrimp turns white and loses its translucent character. Repeat this process for the chicken, which is also cooked in two batches.

Heat the refried beans and the black beans in separate pots over low heat until warmed (approximately 20 minutes). History has taught us that you can't have beans without rice.

Besides, rice is a great filler food to really stretch that burrito bar. Using the white rice of your choice, boil enough water to make four cups of rice. Remember, instant rice is typically a 1 cup rice to 1 cup water kind of affair, bring to a boil, add rice, and then let steam for about 5 minutes. "Real" rice is usually a 1½ cup water to 1 cup rice ratio. Bring water to a boil, add rice and let simmer, covered, for about twenty minutes or until tender. As always, don't take our word for it, check the instructions on the box or bag of the specific rice which you have purchased. Finally, cut the bell peppers and onions into thin, bite-sized strips; sauté the peppers and onions separately in the cooking oil in a nonstick skillet, over low heat, for 10 minutes or until the onions are translucent. Place the contents of both pots of beans, rice, the bell peppers, and the onions in individual serving bowls and move them to the food table. Likewise the shredded Monterey Jack and fat-free sour cream.

Preheat the oven to 350 degrees. Give each corn tortilla a short squirt of cooking spray to wet the surface. Place each in a large piece of aluminum foil. Repeat until you have a stack of twenty tortillas. Wrap the foil over the top. Repeat until all the tortillas are stacked and wrapped. Heat the tortilla stacks for 10 minutes in the ovens.

When designing the food table layout, you need to remember that people are making their own burritos. They will need a plate, then the tortilla, shrimp or chicken, and condiments in that order. So be sure to arrange your table to keep each guest moving and the food line short.

Guacamole

While your tortillas are heating, make your fresh homemade Guacamole.

3 ripe avocados
3 Roma tomatoes
3 cloves fresh garlic
2 bunches fresh cilantro, chopped
3 tablespoons jalapeño-style Tabasco
Salt and pepper to taste

Slice the three avocados in half and use a melon baller to scoop out the ripe meat. Place the avocado "balls" in a large bowl. Slice the three Roma tomatoes into quarters and rinse out the moisture and seeds. Chop the tomatoes into tiny pieces and add them to the bowl. Use a garlic press for those three cloves of fresh garlic. It's so much faster. Add the garlic to the bowl. Add the chopped cilantro, jalapeño Tabasco, and salt and pepper. Although Brooksie sometimes adds a little fresh chopped red onion, we don't see a reason for adding to the bad breath factor at this point, so you can skip it and move on to mixing the Guacamole. Use a potato masher to thoroughly mix all the ingredients in the bowl. Brooksie's technique involves thrusting the masher up and down while simultaneously spinning the bowl in a circle. But you want the Guacamole to have a thick and hearty consistency, so this should only take about a minute.

Salsa

Four 16-ounce jars ready-made
red salsas (two hot and two mild)
Four 8-ounce bags tortilla chips
(a nice selection of blue corn, yellow corn,
and red if available)

While we could give a recipe for homemade salsa, we won't. First, you just spent like 5 whole minutes making that awesome Guacamole, which everyone will be raving about. Second, it requires your blender, and you need to save that for your margaritas. So just put your store-bought salsas into some pretty serving dishes and hide the jars they came in. If anyone compliments you on your fantastic salsa recipe, just smile and say "Thank you."

Next, open a bag or two of your chips and place in a bowl near your salsa and Guacamole. There you go. Chips and dips.

Tequila Lime Mousse

This menu requires you to work backward as your Tequila Lime Mousse will need to chill for 2 hours before it can be served. If you happen to own an electric mixer with a wire whisk attachment, you are in luck, because it makes this recipe so much easier. Should you lack the big mixer with fun attachments, fear not, you can still make this recipe, just use a large bowl and a wire whisk to mix it together. In either case, it's easier to make it in two equally divided batches, because two tubs of reduced-fat Cool Whip is a lot of Cool Whip.

Two 3-ounce packages sugar-free lime gelatin
1⅓ cups boiling water
1 cup chilled tequila
1 cup very cold water (with 2 or 3
ice cubes per ½ cup)
Two 8-ounce tubs reduced-fat Cool Whip

Start by opening a package of sugar-free gelatin and placing it in a bowl. Add ⅔ cup of the boiling water and stir rapidly until the gelatin dissolves. Next, add ½ cup of the chilled tequila and ½ cup of the very cold water with the ice cubes. Continue stirring until the ice cubes melt. Add one tub of the Cool Whip and use either an electric mixer with a wire whisk attachment or a wire whisk to blend the Cool Whip into the gelatin-tequila-water mixture. Mix until the Cool Whip is a lovely mint green color. Chill for 2 hours in the refrigerator. Repeat this process to make the second batch, because everyone will want to try your Mexican dessert, which looks so much more appealing than a flan.

Margaritas

You're doing a lot of cooking for this party. Why complicate matters further worrying if you added too much triple sec? Just opt for a basic premix and add the tequila. The standard ratio is 3 ounces of premix for every 1.5 ounces of tequila. We'll even leave the great question of frozen versus on the rocks up to you. We do, however, insist that you place a bowl of freshly cut lime wedges and a container of margarita salt next to the pitcher or punch bowl of margaritas. For details on our great margarita taste test, read "A Word About . . . " at the end of this chapter.

MAKE THE MOOD COME ALIVE

The music is all about Latin pop—the Gipsy Kings, Shakira, Mark Anthony, Selena, Los Lobos, Ricky Martin.[1] Or if your cable provider has it, just set the TV on MTV Latin.

If unfilled at purchase, fill your piñatas with the traditional candy and little trinkets, and before too many margaritas have been consumed, play break the piñata. While you may be kind of sad to see your decorations go, it's a great ice breaker activity, and it'll get the crowd mixing. Besides, even after the piñatas are gone, everyone will still be talking about how cute they were and what a great idea it was.

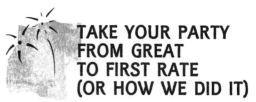

TAKE YOUR PARTY FROM GREAT TO FIRST RATE (OR HOW WE DID IT)

Liven up your food table even more by using a sombrero to hold the chips and margarita glasses for the dips.

Add more detail to the bathroom. Put a small bowl of Mexican jumping beans on the vanity.

If you took your Mardi Gras Party from great to first rate, you probably have some leftover green crepe paper. Use it to accent your party space. Simply start by taping one end up

---

1. You know at least five people that have at least one of these CDs.

high in the corner of your room, draping it to the center, but allowing it to hang about 18 inches from the ceiling.

Be the tequila sheriff. Almost every bar in Tijuana has the waiter who roves around the bar wearing a holster that contains a bottle of tequila. Typically, one of your friends will give him $2.00 to come over and give you a tequila shooter. He pours the tequila directly into your mouth and then shakes your head a few times. If you're lucky, he'll rub a little lime juice and salt on your hand to take the edge off. Make your party come alive and be that annoying waiter or designate a guest to do so. If you're single, you can use it as an excuse to kiss the cute boys at the party by charging a kiss a shooter.

TIMELINE

Cinco de Mayo is always as the name denotes— the fifth of May. Unfortunately, this date is not always ideal for a party. Should the fifth of May fall on a date when entertaining would be inconvenient, select the Friday or Saturday night prior to the big day and your party will help to add momentum to the actual celebration.

Also keep in mind that while the menu is fairly simple, there's a lot of sautéing to be done. Consider asking a friend to help you with the setup. By now, someone is dying to learn your party secrets, so find a *co-chair* and start training her.

Two weeks before the party—Send out your e-mail invitation.

One week before the party—Inventory your leftover party decorations to see what can be recycled and what must be purchased. Shop for any needed decorations and paper goods. Make your luminarias.

The night before the party—Tidy up your party space. If you are using a patio or deck for the first time this year, you may need to hose down or clean off furniture and sweep the space out.

The morning of the party—Since you're celebrating Mexican independence, declare your independence from the razor and have a bikini wax. Besides, the pool opens at the end of the month, so you need to start doing this anyway. Stop by the grocery and/or liquor store on the way home to shop. We also recommend you start drinking insane amounts of water as tequila can be very dehydrating.

The afternoon of the party—Don't forget your preparty nap.

4 P.M.	Make the Tequila Lime Mousse dessert.
5 P.M.	Decorate your party space. Begin to set up the food table.
6 P.M.	Make the first pitcher of margaritas. Naturally, you should try the first one to make sure it tastes O.K. as you begin to sauté the shrimp and chicken. Make Guacamole.
6:30 P.M.	Finish your hair and makeup.

6:40 P.M.	Make rice, heat the beans, and sauté the vegetables. Start heating tortillas.
6:50 P.M.	Lay out your food table to celebrate the rich heritage of Mexico and maximize party flow. Put out chips and dips.
7 P.M.	Light the luminarias and greet your guests as they arrive.
8 P.M.	Start whacking the hell out of those piñatas!

A WORD ABOUT . . . MARGARITA TASTE TESTING

In the eternal quest for perfection in party planning, we conducted a thorough margarita taste test. The research design scared nearly all the men we know and also provided an opportunity to verify the slogan "feel better than you should," as advertised by Alka-Seltzer Morning Relief. We compared three premade margarita mixes available at our local liquor retailer, a homemade concoction composed of sour mix and orange juice, and then one mix we labeled as "leftovers." All mixes were sampled twice, once with Jose Cuervo Gold Tequila and then made with Jose Cuervo White Tequila. Each drink was rated in the following categories: price, number of servings per bottle, ease of preparation, color, calories per serving, sweetness, tartness, and overall taste.

Given the level of detail devoted to designing the research methodology, we really wish we could provide our results herein. But a funny thing happens when you settle in to personally drink ten margaritas in one night. We've coined "marga-amnesia" as a clinical term to describe our inability to remember anything past the sixth margarita. Even our notes kind of trail off at that point. Brooksie vaguely recalls liking the drink labeled "leftover with white Jose," but Morgan was bartending and can't remember what premixes she combined to make it.

We don't recommend you try replicating this taste test at home. In hindsight, we consider this idea as taking one for the team. Should you ever decide that home experimentation is needed to reveal the ingredients used to make your favorite cocktail, we urge you to reconsider. Instead, just go to the bar where you like the way the cocktail tastes, and ask the bartender how they make it. This approach may not seem as much fun, but it's cost effective and may potentially prevent the loss of brain cells that could occur should the experiment go awry.

Chapter Six

JUNE, JULY, and AUGUST

THE ULTIMATE ROAD TRIP

Come on, baby, take a ride with me.

CONCEPT

Wanderlust seems to bite everyone in the summer. So instead of planning a bunch of big parties that half your friends will miss because of their vacations, grab two or three *pledge sisters* and hit the road yourself.

We realize that the words road trip bring to mind different destinations for everyone. For your faithful founders, only the beach will do. But don't let us limit you. Call your state's tourism bureau to get some ideas you might not have considered. Then follow these easy "do's and don'ts" for a great adventure.

WHAT AN RSG WOULD DO . . .

Do invite reliable *pledge sisters*. We realize that everyone is busy, but you are basing your trip on a budget. If someone cancels at the last minute, everyone else ends up with a slightly higher than-agreed-to tab.

Do be flexible. Try to accommodate everyone, whether it's the music selection, different meals, or tourist traps. People are generally willing to compromise as long as they are getting their way at least some of the time.

Do plan. Make reservations ahead. Many hotels, especially near beaches and resorts, fill up quickly. You don't want to waste valuable vacation time looking for a bed or contemplating how all of you will sleep in the car.

Do hype the road trip. Part of the fun is the expectation.

Do be silly. Singing along to Brittany Spears or playing the license plate game as you drive to the beach makes the miles fly. Remember, what happens on the road, stays on the road.

Do be the *social chair*. As the road trip organizer, you are a traveling hostess. Try to anticipate people's various needs such as sunblock, bug spray, Handi Wipes, etc. If someone forgets something, you'll either have to make an emergency stop, or that person will suffer and be unhappy. Neither option is ideal, so anticipate to avoid problems.

Do plan a traffic strategy. Understand your area's traffic patterns and do your best to avoid sitting in bumper-to-bumper traffic. Most people hate traffic and are willing to get up early to avoid it. Besides, when putting several different personalities in the same car for a few hours, you are bound to have disagreements. Avoid anything that will cause tempers to flare before you've reached your destination.

Do plan to do nothing. Everyone needs a certain amount of "me" time. Sitting on the beach, half asleep, half awake, gives everyone that time they need to recharge and reenergize.

Do split the work. Have someone in charge of snacks, someone in charge of music, someone in charge of booze, etc. It fosters *sisterhood* and takes some of the organizing burdens off you.

Do find an equitable way to split expenses. It's easiest for you as the organizer to put the hotel room on your credit card when you make reservations. Make sure people know approximately how much the expenses will be before they commit to the trip.

WHAT AN RSG WOULD NEVER DO . . .

Don't go too far. Anything over 4 hours in the car is probably too far, especially if it's a small car and you have four people in it.

Don't be rigid. Everyone has different expectations for the trip. Plan to accommodate.

Don't be afraid to try something new. This is a road trip—you've got to take advantage of new experiences.

Don't forget the camera. Having pictures to show afterward will bolster your *social chair* reputation, and can easily double as simple Christmas gifts for your fellow road-trippers when you creatively frame them.

Don't talk on the cell phone unless it's to confirm reservations or find a destination. Focus on your *pledge sisters*.

Don't forget that some resort areas charge higher prices for necessities like bottled water and film. Plan ahead so you don't pay through the nose.

Don't forget to have fun! A little spontaneity can lead to the best stories!

RED-HOT
FOURTH OF JULY
POTLUCK

Celebrate your party freedom!

CONCEPT

Declare your independence! Take a break from the traditional, and somewhat tired, Fourth of July cookout by hosting a potluck to celebrate America's favorite foods. In addition to creating an alternative menu for the Fourth, you'll also be declaring your independence from the kitchen and meat that tastes like lighter fluid.

Using the Fourth of July for your party theme makes creating an original party more difficult than many of the other party plans outlined in this book. It's an important day for our nation and its citizens, but surprisingly there are no music or movies or games anyone under sixty will enjoy directly connected to the day. At best, most families have formed their own personal traditions based around supermarket discounts on hotdogs and hamburgers. We would hope that a true RSG *sister* would never pollute her body with a discount hotdog. For that reason, we invite you to embrace the theme of independence and give your guests a day filled with freedom of choice and an easy culinary tour of America. Can you really get more American than that?

We can't guarantee this concept will be immediately accepted with open arms. But think of the adversity that our Founding Fathers faced as they grappled with the concept of inalienable rights.[1] They overcame it through organization, compromise, and hard work. We'll show you how to do the same, minus the hard work.

DECORATIONS

1 American flag, any size that you can display respectfully.

1 red-and-white-checked tablecloth, plus more if needed

30 paper or plastic red, white, or blue plates

40 red, white, or blue napkins

30 sets of plastic cutlery

40 red, white, or blue plastic cups

One 42-feet package of red crepe paper

One 42-feet package of navy blue crepe paper

1 roll of Scotch tape

The party colors are a no-brainer. Your colors are red, white, and blue. Make sure to display the flag in a respectful, yet prominent manner.

An outdoor party space is truly essential for the day, so if you don't have a backyard or large balcony, consider renting picnic space at a local park. Most cities offer discounted rates to residents.

Your red-and-white-checked tablecloth returns to cover the food table. Should you decide to hold your party at a local park, a few extra plastic tablecloths will be needed to cover dirty picnic tables previously used by the masses and will add a nice personal touch.

Recycle any red or white plates, napkins, cups, and cutlery you might have. To fill in the gaps and maintain balance in your party space, purchase the needed items in blue.

Attach the red and blue crepe paper with Scotch tape to make railings, fences, and posts stand out. You should also drape a twist of the two colors around your food table to give it a bunting look.

---

1. Although the Founding Fathers were not fraternity men, they were members of similar organizations. George Washington was a Freemason!

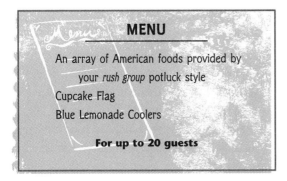

MENU

An array of American foods provided by
your *rush group* potluck style

Cupcake Flag

Blue Lemonade Coolers

For up to 20 guests

 **FOOD**

When we said celebrate freedom from the kitchen, we meant it. This party is potluck! Your potluck should celebrate American foods— whether it's a hometown favorite or a specialty derived from America's melting pot. Encourage your guests to bring a dish that will highlight a specific region or culinary tradition. So many people move from one region of the country to another, one of the things they always seem to miss most about "home" is some type of food item or preparation that can seemingly only be done correctly in a certain obscure restaurant from their region of origin. Who doesn't know a North Carolina transplant frantically searching

New York or the Midwest for a decent pulled pork sandwich? Or a Louisiana transplant who seems utterly flummoxed at the lack of authentic-tasting jambalaya in his or her new home? So, challenge your guests to share a little of their heritage, be it regional or international. The result should be a unique menu showcasing the diversity that makes America great.

But coordinating it will take a little work. If you invite over ten people, you may want to assign food types, i.e., A–F bring entrées, G–V bring side dishes, and W–Z bring nonalcoholic beverages. Make sure people commit to their dish when they RSVP.[2]

Your faithful founders believe there's nothing like the spirit of competition to generate preparty buzz, so consider offering prizes for various dishes. The electronic invitation should include this incentive, as well as a direction that people select what type of dish they will be bringing. We enjoyed awarding "Most Traditional," "Should've Stayed in the Old World," and "I'd Even Go to Memphis for Barbecue Like That." As always, your faithful founders strongly recommend you award a prize to the guy you have a crush on, even if his homemade Swedish meatballs tasted like cardboard.

2. If people do not tell you their dish when they RSVP, you have our permission to hunt them down and hound them.

Cupcake Flag

As hostess, you will provide dessert—cupcakes depicting the Stars and Stripes. The cupcake flag is pure genius. It provides a strong visual impact and highlights your creativity but really requires minimal effort on your part and also provides you with a stunning centerpiece for your food table.

Two 18.25-ounce boxes cake mix
    (yellow, white, chocolate, or
    a combination of two flavors)
One 3-ounce box blue raspberry Jell-O
One 16-ounce can strawberry frosting
One 16-ounce standard package
    white chocolate chips
One 16-ounce can white chocolate frosting
3 to 4 drops blue food coloring (optional)
½ teaspoon powdered sugar (optional)
Two 2½-inch packages silver, standard-size
    cupcake wrappers (at least 40)

According to the directions on the boxes of cake mix bake at least forty standard-sized cupcakes in the silver baking tins. No matter how many the package yields, you will only be using forty for your flag. Once the cupcakes have cooled, arrange them on a baking sheet in a 5 by 8 rectangle. The flag effect will be created by applying different icing to different sections of the flag.

Pour about one teaspoon of the Jell-O mix in a small bowl. Add only enough water to dissolve the Jell-O. Then, mix in enough of the white chocolate frosting to ice 6 cupcakes. You may want to deepen the blue with food coloring and also add additional powdered sugar to prevent running. Once you have made your blue raspberry icing, ice the leftmost two cupcakes in the top three rows of your flag. This will make a six-cupcake blue field. Add the fifty white chocolate chip "stars," eight on four cupcakes and nine on two.

Next, you will ice the lower two rows of eight cupcakes and the upper three rows of six cupcakes. Alternate the white chocolate and strawberry icing to make the thirteen red and white stripes as you ice the five rows of remaining cupcakes. For the top and bottom rows, the cupcakes will be two tone, one stripe strawberry and one stripe white chocolate. For the middle three rows, there will be three stripes per cupcake. Starting from the top, begin with a strawberry stripe for the top half of the top row of six. Next ice the bottom half of those cupcakes in white chocolate.

Proceeding to the next row of six, ice the top one-third of that row's cupcakes with strawberry, the middle one-third of each cupcake in that row with white chocolate, and the bottom one-third of each cupcake in that row with strawberry. For the last row of six it will be top one-third white chocolate, middle one-third strawberry, and bottom one-third white chocolate.

For the first row of eight, you will be making your final set of top one-third strawberry, middle one-third white chocolate, and bottom one-third strawberry cupcakes. For the bottom row, ice only two stripes. The top stripe should be white chocolate and the bottom should be strawberry.

Varying the icing flavors while presenting an accurate thirteen stripes and fifty stars takes your dessert from fun and great to flavor filled and first rate. Another way to make your cupcake flag even more special is to vary the cake flavors as well as the icing flavors. While yellow cake works very well with the blue raspberry icing, using chocolate with some of your striped white chocolate/strawberry creations can be, for cupcakes, a very sophisticated touch.

Blue Lemonade Coolers

Brooksie has long been fascinated by blue drinks and believes they should be embraced by America. The recipe here is a vast improvement over the swill she used to make in her dorm in college. The refreshing blend of lemonade and seltzer offer a temporary respite from the summer heat while carrying forward colors of the party.

Four .22-ounce envelopes Ice Blue Raspberry Lemonade Kool-Aid

4 cups sugar

Two 2-liter bottles lemon-flavored seltzer

Four 1-liter bottles Absolut Citron vodka

Two 32-ounce jars maraschino cherries for garnish

Since you'll be enjoying the great outdoors, it's best to make this cocktail in a very large cooler, preferably one with a spout. But since we don't know how large your cooler is, we'll make the coolers one envelope of Kool-Aid at a time. Begin by making the Kool-Aid, which is the contents of the packet, one cup of sugar, and 2 quarts of water. Add one liter of lemon-flavored seltzer and 1 liter of Absolut Citron Vodka. Repeat until your cooler is full.

This drink is best served over ice, so be sure to devote a second cooler to this purpose. You'll need about four large (8-pound) bags. Garnish each glass of Blue Lemonade Cooler with a maraschino cherry and toast to our nation's independence.

MAKE THE MOOD COME ALIVE

Keep local traditions and events in mind when planning your Fourth of July party. Is there a parade that draws a big crowd? When and where are the big fireworks displays? What do people in your town typically do? You need to tie these factors into your party. We suggest starting the party around 4 P.M., so that it will wrap up around 8 P.M. or so. This allows you and your guests to go see the fireworks if they cannot be viewed from your party site.

It's hot. It's probably a long day for most people. And if the Fourth falls on Monday through Thursday, people have to work the next day. Bottom line, you should probably keep the mayhem to a minimum, but still provide some activity options to help mix different groups of people and spark conversation. We suggest traditional summertime favorites like croquet, badminton, and horseshoes. If your guests have an affinity for one of these "sports," arrange a tournament. Keep in mind, teams force different individuals to talk to each other. If you are going to have small children and some heavy drinkers, we discourage you from selecting lawn darts as an option. In fact, the official RSG *risk management* policy states that lawn darts are prohibited at events where alcohol is served. (See, e.g., Rho Sigma Gamma *Risk Management* policy, section 3(b)(iii)).

Despite our deep-seated belief in maintaining the party's theme at all times, your faithful founders are not really picky about the music for this party. Unless your *rush group* is really into classical music and wants to hear the 1812 Overture all day, there's not a lot of music that really connects itself to the Fourth of July. So, just play whatever most of your friends usually listen to, whether it's Top 40, country, or classic rock. Again, you're embracing your independence with this party, so you make the music selection.

TAKE YOUR PARTY FROM GREAT TO FIRST RATE (OR HOW WE DID IT)

Add some cohesion to the food table by using several small American flags to decorate. Make labels for all the dishes by listing the name of the guest who provided it, the name of the dish, and the guest's hometown.

Incorporate a water element to combat the heat. Whether it's sprinklers for the kids to play in or misters to cool the adults, it'll be appreciated.

Provide your guests with a few extra amenities necessitated by the great outdoors. Sunscreen, insect repellent, and citronella candles will be welcomed.

Where legal, provide sparklers for all your guests.

TIMELINE

Here's where the American value of organization becomes important. In order to present a well-balanced array of American dishes, you need to foster the spirit of cooperation and preparty buzz simultaneously. Luckily, the reply-all feature on your e-mail is a tool that makes this easy. But you must also keep in mind that the Fourth of July is a popular beach weekend, so it's best to announce your plans earlier, rather than later. We suggest sending your electronic invitation out three weeks prior to the party.

Four plus weeks before the party—If you plan to have your party at a local park, reserve the space now.

Three weeks before the party—Send out the e-mail invitation.

One week before the party—Follow up with any guests who replied with interest, but did not tell you what kind of dish they plan to bring. Inventory your paper products and purchase any you are lacking. Purchase decorations.

The day before the party—Do your grocery and liquor shopping.

The morning of the party—Make the cupcakes. Get in a festive spirit by painting your nails red. Remember, you can be theme-appropriate and still satisfy your inner vixen.

3 P.M.	Decorate the party space. Set up lawn games.
3:30 P.M.	Make Blue Lemonade Coolers.
4 P.M.	Greet your guests with, "Happy Independence Day!"

A WORD ABOUT . . . ALCOHOL AND FIREWORKS

While the Rho Sigma Gamma *Risk Management* Policy prohibits mixing lawn darts and alcohol at section 3(b)(iii), section 3(b)(i) deals with an even more important prohibition: mixing alcohol and fireworks. Now, we could discourage you from mixing alcohol and fireworks by showing you pictures of people who chose this combination. But they aren't pretty. So instead, we'll just firmly caution you.

Although fireworks for personal purchase are legal in many jurisdictions and are frequently used as fund-raisers for local organizations, some cities do restrict the private use of fireworks. Further, use of fireworks when conditions have been dry can result in an unexpected lawn or brushfire, and in our experience, an unexpected fire sucks more than just the oxygen out of its path; it'll suck the life of your party with it. And if you've ever had to explain why something has happened to a law enforcement officer after you have consumed four Blue Lemonade Coolers, you may suddenly find yourself unable to stop hiccuping, laughing, slurring, or some other equally awkward combination. Handcuffs may be involved, and not in the good way.

In many cases, fireworks are one of those things that just sound cooler than they really are. To use them safely, you need to take specific precautions, such as having a fire extinguisher within reach, etc. If your party is fun the fireworks will come from the guests, not from a tent by the highway.

We suggest you simply leave the fireworks to the professionals and just ooh and ahh instead of asking, "Did that light?"

And in case you were wondering, section 3(b)(ii) of the Rho Sigma Gamma *Risk Management* policy is never mix alcohol with ex-boyfriends. On the hierarchy of danger, the flow is clear. Ex-boyfriends are less dangerous than fireworks, but obviously, deadlier than lawn darts. When you must choose, opt for the alcohol. The booze never cheated on you with your *sister*.

END-OF-SUMMER POOL PARTY

Cool off with a dip in the pool,

and then heat things up in your bikini!

CONCEPT

Just because summer is almost over doesn't mean you can't make time for one last fling. End the summer with the hottest, yet coolest, social event—a pool party, grown-up style.

But you're freaking out because you don't have a pool! Don't worry, that's why God invented Slip 'n Slides. Now that you don't live with your parents (at least we hope you don't) no one will complain about the damage to the grass. However, we do suggest you consult legal counsel and enclose waivers with the invitations.

Why a pool party? Because everyone clings to the last vestige of summer, everyone fondly remembers those junior high summer vacations, when you were too young to work, but too old to require a baby-sitter. Translation: Days filled with all the fun you could hide before 5 P.M. when Mom got home. But you're grown up now, so it's all the fun you can hide before 5 A.M.—or whenever that old man next door calls the cops.

Faithful *rushees*, the most important trait every member of RSG possesses is her party vision. We've already re-created the hottest club in Havana with Cabin Fever Beach Party and a Los Cabos–style resort for Cinco de Mayo. Clearly this party must be different, and it is. Now is the time to infuse a little good old American fun into your *rush group*'s party experience, so think Jersey shore or Outer Banks, North Carolina.

Don't get freaked about your friends and coworkers seeing you in your bathing suit. That's not what this party is about. Focus on the idea of good, warm carefree days and trying to remember how to perform a quality cannonball. Besides they sell really cute matching sarongs with bathing suits these days—and don't forget the matching flip-flops.

The crest of the Society of Recovering

DECORATIONS

An assortment of beach towels—all the ones you own, you may even want to borrow a few

3 to 5 inflatable beach balls

1 large Mexican blanket

10 luminarias from Cinco de Mayo party

10 plain white votive candles (if new candles are needed)

Two 40-pound bags of sand

2 Slip 'n Slides (use *only* if you have no pool)

1 small kiddie pool—inflatable or plastic—get what's on sale

1 to 2 large citronella candles

12 tiki torches

Citronella fuel

White Christmas tree lights

Curling ribbon

Volleyball net—if you're using a pool

Ubiquitous box or glass of shells you have from your last vacation

One 8-ounce bottle of sunscreen per 20 guests (chilled) preferably with an SPF of 30 or higher

30 paper or plastic plates; select a color that matches your beach towels or yellow to match the Slip 'n Slides

40 paper napkins; select a color that matches your beach towels or yellow to match the Slip 'n Slides

30 sets of plastic cutlery

40 plastic cups; select a color that matches your beach towels or yellow to match the Slip 'n Slides

END-OF-SUMMER POOL PARTY **121**

Sorority Girls contains two words, *recycalda* and *attitudium*. These words hail from Old Latin and are sacred to your faithful founders as they encompass our most strongly held ideals: You can do anything with what you've got, as long as you know how to commit to the appropriate mind-set. Any a-hole can invite people over to the house for hotdogs and a jump in the pool. Don't be that girl. While others serve carnival fare, you provide an upscale salad and wrap bar. While others think a simple pool is entertainment enough, you provide beach balls and a sandy faux beach. And if you don't have a pool, you have the attitude that empowers you to convince your friends that sliding headfirst down a glorified, yellow garbage bag is the greatest thing since sliced bread. These principles have allowed our organization to grow and to flourish. In addition, they support our most fundamental belief: Home entertaining is not a job—it's a low-stress adventure.

We'll begin specific instructions with the first word contained in our crest, *recycalda*. You may note that the first several decorations listed were all used at the Cabin Fever Beach Party. Yes, you're using them again. Only this time,

use the beach towels for drying off your guests and the beach balls can go directly in the pool. The Mexican blanket and luminarias return from Cinco de Mayo. Once you reassemble the luminarias, line your walkway with them. The blanket returns to the food table as a reward for its washability and the fact it's August and like ninety degrees. Who wants to sit on a blanket when there's water to splash in?

If there's water to be had, it's imperative to play in it. Unfortunately, most of us live in landlocked communities and very few of us know the pleasure of waking up and gazing out on the crystal blue water. But for a primal reason we cannot fathom, the sight of water is instantly calming, focusing and reminding us all of one hell of a good time. Speaking of one hell of a good time, *attitudium* means taking a common everyday party and turning it into something your guests will remember forever. So fear not—if you don't have a pool, the Slip 'n Slides meet the definition of *attitudium* in a valorous and most dignified manner.[3]

We'll move on to lighting. As your party starts in the late afternoon, we recommend you follow Sheryl Crow's advice and "Soak Up the Sun." But soon, that sun will start to slip and

---

3. It is important to note that it takes a very special girl to encourage her friends to fully embrace the greatness that is the Slip 'n Slide. But we wouldn't tell you to do it if weren't great.

you will need a lighting scheme. This is easy as you already have white Christmas tree lights and luminarias. We just ask that you kindly add a citronella candle or two, as well as twelve festive tiki torches arranged surrounding your outdoor table and chairs. Use citronella fuel to protect chatting guests from bugs. Do not set torches in the path of the Slip 'n Slides to protect sliding guests from fire. Now you're all set for nighttime Slip 'n Slide races!

MENU

The temperature alone is already ninety degrees, and that's not including the heat being created by you in your bikini. Serve a menu that can cool things down a bit—an upscale salad and wraps bar.

Mesclun Salad
Fruit Salad
Asian Noodle Salad
Roasted Turkey Club Wraps
Chips and Salsa
Pink Flamingo

For up to 20 guests

Mesclun Salad

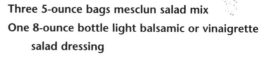

Three 5-ounce bags mesclun salad mix
One 8-ounce bottle light balsamic or vinaigrette salad dressing

Open the bags of salad mix, and place the greens in a serving bowl. Toss lightly with the balsamic or vinaigrette dressing. Dispose of the empty salad mix bags in a garbage can so that no one will find it. This is an upscale dish, but no one needs to know how easy it was.

Fruit Salad

You'll save some valuable sunblock application time by preparing the fruit salad the night before the party. While the recipe is super summertime easy, the chopping will take about 30 minutes.

2 red apples, cored and chopped into ½-inch cubes
2 green apples, cored and chopped into ½-inch cubes
½ pound strawberries, cleaned and chopped into small pieces
¼ pound red seedless grapes, cut in half
¼ pound green seedless grapes, cut in half

¼ **pound chopped walnuts**

1 **lemon**

1 **tablespoon cornstarch**

¼ **cup sugar**

**One 15½-ounce can pineapple tidbits with
their juice**

Begin by washing and cutting up all the fruit, except the pineapple tidbits. Place the nuts and all the fruit except the pineapple in either a resealable bowl or go ahead and use your serving dish, but plan to cover it with plastic wrap. Drain the juice from the can of pineapple tidbits, reserving the juice for use in the dressing. Add the pineapple tidbits to the rest of the fruit.

The hard part is over. Let's make the dressing. Pour the pineapple juice into a saucepan. Cut the lemon into halves and squeeze the juice from the lemon into the pan. Add the cornstarch and sugar. Cook on low heat, stirring frequently. The dressing should start to thicken. After about 10 minutes, remove the saucepan from the heat and pour the dressing over the fruit and nuts. Immediately begin stirring the fruit to evenly distribute the dressing. Stir thoroughly, about 90 seconds. Cover and store in the fridge until the party!

Some people will tell you just to get a watermelon and serve it wedge style. But we know you're so much better than that. It's the combination of fruits that make it a real salad, and the pineapple-based dressing gives it a heartier composition. So embrace the upscale in your salad and wraps bar.

Asian Noodle Salad

1 **pound shrimp, shelled and deveined**

1 **pound sugar snap peas**

1 **red bell pepper, seeded and diced into very
small pieces**

1 **cup reduced-sodium soy sauce**

1 **cup reduced-fat creamy peanut butter**

½ **cup sesame oil**

½ **cup brown sugar**

½ **cup rice wine vinegar**

Crushed red pepper to taste

2 **to 3 teaspoons olive oil**

2 **pounds somen noodles (see Note for
more information)**

½ **cup finely chopped fresh cilantro**

Fill a large pot of water, set the burner on high, and bring the water to a boil. While waiting for the water to boil, do the following:

If you are using frozen shrimp and sugar snap peas, rinse thoroughly with cold water to thaw. Quickly cook shrimp and snow peas by sautéing in a skillet with cooking spray. Finely dice the red bell pepper.

Make the dressing by combining the soy sauce, peanut butter, sesame oil, brown sugar, and rice wine vinegar in a large bowl. Whisk until thoroughly combined. Sprinkle with the crushed red pepper to taste.

If you are not pressed for time, consider boiling the noodles in three batches. Once the water begins to boil, add a teaspoon of the olive oil and about half the noodles. While somen noodles are very yummy and cook in about 4 minutes, they're tricky little devils and will stick together at the drop of a hat. Strain and rinse with cold water for about 5 minutes. As you are rinsing the noodles, run your hands through them to further separate them. Big chunks of noodles congealed together are bad.

Place the noodles in a large bowl with a lid, add the shrimp, cilantro, sugar snap peas, red bell pepper, and dressing. Put the lid on and shake to mix. Refrigerate overnight. Prior to serving, give the container a few more good shakes to keep everything mixed together. Serve chilled.

Note: If somen noodles aren't available, use angel hair pasta.

Roasted Turkey Club Wraps

No one eats bread anymore, so don't you serve it.

30 tomato-flavored flour tortillas
30 slices roasted turkey breast
30 slices cooked turkey bacon
1 large red onion, chopped
One 16-ounce jar spicy brown or Grey Poupon mustard

Take one tomato-flavored tortilla and spread some spicy mustard on it. On the left side of the tortilla place one slice of roasted turkey meat. Top it with one slice of turkey bacon and ½ teaspoon of the chopped red onion. Next, roll the wrap from left to right as you would sushi. If you don't remember how to do this, reread the Japanese Cherry Blossom Festival. The mustard will keep the roll together. Make one diagonal cut near the center of the roll and you will have two "sandwich" segments to serve. Repeat to make 60 segments.

Chips and Salsa

Two 13.5-ounce large bags tortilla chips—use colored if they match your beach towels
Two 16-ounce jars of salsa, one hot, one mild

As always, liberate the chips. Free them from the captivity that is the bag. Empty the salsa into serving bowls.

Pink Flamingo

Our comprehensive research for a signature cocktail designed to truly evoke the sense and feel of this party came up short. Seriously, how do you say "Slip 'n Slide" race through a beverage? We decided to invent our own concoction, which screams lack of adult supervision. We call it the Pink Flamingo. The recipe is simple.

3.5 liters mango rum
Three 46-ounce cans pineapple juice
One 12-ounce bottle grenadine

Combine 2 ounces of mango rum, 2 ounces of pineapple juice, and ½ teaspoon of grenadine in a cocktail shaker with ice. Shake, strain, and enjoy. Hmm, it's yummy. But for party purposes, we recommend you make approximately twenty Pink Flamingos the night before and freeze them in a plastic container, making a fabulous cocktail Popsicle that will chill your punch bowl. Thirty minutes before your guests arrive, remove the container of frozen Pink Flamingos from the freezer and dump it in the punch bowl. Now you don't have to worry about ice watering down your drinks on a hot day.

Since your "ice" is in the punch bowl, you can make the punch. If your cocktail shaker is large enough, double the recipe above and make enough to fill your punch bowl. While using the shaker does take a little time, its results are superior to any other method. And again, you don't have any ice watering down your drink. If you get tired of shaking, just ask some guy to help you. No one ever says no to the hostess!

Just a short discussion about your food table. While placing it outside in the prime party space may seem appropriate, the sun and heat will do really mean things to your salads. And since nothing says bad party like food poisoning, just keep the food table in the kitchen or appropriately air-conditioned space off the deck or patio. By prerolling sets of plastic cutlery in a napkin and securing with a piece of curling ribbon, it's still possible for guests to carry a plate and drink outside with minimal juggling.

MAKE THE MOOD COME ALIVE

Music. We have two words—world beat. Think reggae, think salsa, think tropical. If you have digital cable, you'll have four channels in your music selection to choose from. We like the Brazilian pop channel and Tropicale.

Flip cup is a game we discovered in the woods of northern New Jersey. The object of the game is, well, there is no object. But the idea is a drinking game race. You assemble your guests into teams with each team having at least three members. Team members then pour a shot quantity of the beverage of their choice into their plastic cup. The first member of each team drinks a shot as quickly as the person can and places the cup back on the picnic table so that half the bottom of the cup hangs over the edge of the picnic table. Then, you tap the bottom of the cup with two to three fingers of your hand in a manner designed to "flip" the cup over onto its mouth, so that it is upside down on the picnic table. Once the cup lands in that position, the next team member drinks a shot and the process is repeated. In the event that you fail to properly flip your cup, you must continue to attempt the flip until you do. The result is a competitive race highlighting the effects of alcohol on your reflexes. We warn you, depending on how many type-A personalities are at your party, Flip Cup can become a blood sport.

Luckily, you can throw them in the pool to cool off—or announce a special Slip 'n Slide victory lap for the winners. We promise that Flip Cup is a positively good time. It beats the game Asshole, which has too many rules, and

we don't recommend adults ever play "I Never." The dominating Flip Cup team is treated to a treasure hunt—bring back the kiddie pool filled with sand. Mix some small, fabulous prizes, such as Canadian money, in the sand-filled pool. Trust us—nothing is funnier than watching drunk people dig around in sand for fabulous prizes.

Meanwhile, in the pool, have a volleyball net set up and put those inflatable beach balls to use. Not everyone will have the physical dexterity for Flip Cup.

So, you've got an intense game of Flip Cup, some volleyball in the pool, and resort-quality cocktails and fine tropical music. Not to mention, half-naked people walking around wet. This is a party!

TAKE YOUR PARTY FROM GREAT TO FIRST RATE (OR HOW WE DID IT)

After much deliberation, we came to a firm conclusion. This party can only be done on the first-rate level. The above list clearly abides by the beliefs of the Society of Recovering Sorority Girls. Whatever you add is a local tradition. We simply ask you notify *national executive office* of said local traditions. Who knows, perhaps we'll adopt them in the next biennium?

TIMELINE

The timeline for this party can be complicated by people's vacation schedules. You don't want guests to miss out on a great party because your e-mail invitation was lost in the jumble of unread e-mails from vacation, so start putting the word out once you decide to host. Because people will still be talking about this party at Christmas, it's O.K. to start planning it a few months in advance. Well, plan is used loosely here. You should start telling people to remember that you are having an end-of-summer pool party when the summer starts.

Three weeks before the party—Send out the e-mail invitation.

Two weeks before the party—Inventory your decorations and determine if there are any holes to be filled.

One week before the party—Begin hydration regimen. Decide which bikini, sarong, and flip-flops you will wear.

The day before the party—Grocery and liquor shop. Make the Fruit Salad and Asian Noodle Salad, and freeze your first batch of Pink Flamingos.

The morning of the party—Tidy up your party space.

2 P.M.	Make sure the pool is ready for visitors or set up the Slip 'n Slides. Set up volleyball net.
3 P.M.	Put on your bikini, sarong, flip-flops, and sunscreen.
3:15 P.M.	Make the turkey wraps.
3:45 P.M.	Make the Mesclun Salad, but don't add the dressing.
4 P.M.	Remove the first batch of Pink Flamingos from the freezer and use as ice as you make the first "official" batch of the cocktails. Greet your guests as they arrive.
5:45 P.M.	Set out salads and add dressing to Mesclun Salad.
6 P.M.	Start the Flip Cup tournament.

A WORD ABOUT . . . PROPER HYDRATION

Nothing spells hangover like dehydration. During the summer months, proper hydration is especially important due to the heat, humidity, and the potential for heat-related illness. While most experts recommend eight 8-ounce glasses of water a day, this is only a recommendation and really doesn't take into account strenuous activity, excessive exposure to the elements, or the dehydrating effects of salty foods, caffeinated beverages, and our good friend, alcohol. For that reason, your faithful founders feel they must remind you to be aware of how much water you are consuming and losing during outdoor events.

During the summer, your preparty rituals should always include becoming properly hydrated. If the party is on Saturday, start drinking the minimum eight 8-ounce glasses of water per day by Monday. As you continue this regimen throughout the week, you'll start to realize it's really not as much water as it sounds, and you may still be thirsty if you spend any time outside. The morning of the party, start drinking water as soon as you get up, as you'll want to have consumed ten 8-ounce glasses before your

first alcoholic beverage. Once you've fortified your system with 80-ounces of water, you are ready to go and only need to rotate in some water every three drinks and after strenuous activity, such as wrestling a man twice your size in a kiddie pool filled with sand for a Canadian quarter. After the party, we strongly recommend you drink a glass of water with three aspirins, or whatever you use to alleviate pain right before going to bed. When selecting your pain reliever, be sure to take note of any warning regarding alcohol on the package.

While proper hydration through drinking water helps keep your skin pretty from the inside out, remember to take care of your skin from the outside in. Moisturize, moisturize, moisturize! We don't care if you look young now, the only way to prevent future wrinkles is moisturizer and sunscreen.

YOU KNOW IT'S TIME FOR A PARTY WHEN . . .

A QUIZ

Please circle every reason you believe merits a party.

1. You have a new outfit.
2. It's your birthday.
3. It's your best friend's birthday.
4. It's winter.
5. It's summer.
6. It's Indian summer.
7. You've been promoted.
8. You've been demoted.
9. You just got engaged.
10. You just got dumped.
11. It's leap year.
12. You achieved your lifelong dream to run a marathon.
13. You won the lottery.
14. You just discovered a unique foreign holiday that merits observance in the United States.
15. It's a bank and federal holiday in the United States.
16. Your mother has announced that she's sick of your father and she's moving to San Francisco with her boyfriend, Mark.
17. Your father has announced he's gay and moving to San Francisco with his boyfriend, Mark.
18. Your parents are celebrating their fiftieth anniversary.
19. It's Tuesday.

20. You've discovered that you are a Recovering Sorority Girl
21. Frankly, every day is a party in my life.

If you circled **sixteen to twenty-one** responses, you're getting a *bid*. We knew it from the moment we met you. Members are jumping up and down, claiming you as their *little sister*. You're the kind of woman who will always make lemonade out of the lemons life throws at her. You already esteem our values, and we're trying to impress you.

If you circled **nine to fifteen** responses, you'll receive an invitation to our *preference party*. We think you have the potential to be a solid member, but we want one last chance to talk about what you are looking for in a sorority. You already know how to celebrate the good things in life, but we worry about how you will respond when the road gets rocky. Will you lean on your *sisters* or retreat?

If you circled **three to eight** responses, you may be invited back to an *invitation only* party. You've clicked with a few members, but more people need to meet you. You also probably need to learn more about Rho Sigma Gamma. Start reading our Web site www.recoveringsororitygirls.com for your monthly party updates and new member education.

If you circled **zero to two** responses, we are cutting you from *rush*. Another sorority may be a better fit for you, but frankly we don't think you're Rho Sigma Gamma material.

If you circled **less than sixteen but more than two** the first time you took this test, read the rest of the book and then retest. We're sure with a little hard "party work" and after careful study of the Rho Sigma Gamma creed, bylaws, and party concepts you'll be able to find more reasons to celebrate!

Chapter Seven

SEPTEMBER

TAILGATE TO TOUCHDOWN

How can a sport that makes men wear pants that tight be bad?

CONCEPT

Although they say baseball is America's pastime, let's face it, nothing captures America's enthusiasm the way football does. Whether it's high school, college, or professional, it ignites a passion and creates a party environment that everyone can enjoy. Who can argue with the singular bliss of grilling a hotdog in a parking lot with your fellow like-minded fans? Without a doubt the star of football season is not that new, cute quarterback or the state champion team, oh no, it's the tailgate!

Although the art of tailgating denotes a parking lot, sport utility vehicle, and ten new best friends, you do have a lot of options. For example, while this party can easily be hosted in any stadium parking lot, its primary principles can also be applied in the comfort of your very own end zone, aka the living room. Your party should be centered on your passion for a specific team and ability/inability to procure tickets.

This party is also formed around a slightly smaller guest list. If you are buying tickets and tailgating at the stadium, keep the difficulties of caravanning in mind. Remember, it's a party, and parties mean leisure so anything stressful is off the menu. And anything more than two car-loads of guests may require extensive cell phone coordination on the road, and who can enjoy that? For tailgating at your home, you should have no more guests than seats around your largest TV. So if the sofa seats three, the chair one, and another three can sit comfortably on cushions on the floor, then six lucky fans plus you will be a sellout.

Hey, don't you dare go turning the page just because you are thinking, "Who cares about some tailgate party? It would require me to understand football." If you don't understand the rules of the game, go to a sports bar during the preseason games, find the hottest guy watching a game and ask him to explain the rules to you. Tell him you are thinking about hosting this party, and he'll be happy to help with your research.[1] This is important because men find women who understand football sexy, and how could you ever not want to be sexy? Besides, even if you don't get it all, your new friend is probably willing to tutor you all season long.

DECORATIONS

All the team logo merchandise you own or can borrow

Napkins, paper plates, paper cups, and plastic utensils in your team's colors

Your decoration plans depend on who you are cheering for—take their colors, and if you can, their mascot too. Get creative! Even if you don't have official logo merchandise of the team you are supporting, it is unacceptable, *rushee*, to not appear in the colors of "your" team. If you are Brooksie, you'll be wearing your Redskins T-shirt, sitting next to your Redskins lamp, with your Redskins blankie draped over your legs. If you are Morgan, you will be draped in your Tampa Bay Buccaneers Beads and wearing appropriate team color wear.[2] Get the picture? This simple decoration scheme works for either venue. Besides, no one will be looking at your decorations with instant replay.

---

1. Both Morgan and Brooksie have found this research method to be useful for many things.
2. If you aren't a true fanatic like Brooksie, or a slave to geography and "hometown" feelings like Morgan, pick the team whose colors best highlight your complexion. Or the team of choice for your cute, male party guests.

Why so little emphasis on decorations? First, if you are at the stadium, you'll have enough to cart out there between food and people. But even if you are tailgating at your home, the emphasis should be on the game, which means people will actually be watching the TV and most conversations will stem from it. Start your party with the pregame show and just leave the TV on. Besides, real football fans will be too engrossed in the game to even notice decorations. The goal is to articulate a theme, not to overdo it!

MENU
_____

Beer Brats
Chips/Pretzels
Precut Veggie Sticks and Dip
S'mores
Flaming Harvey Wallbangers. Haha!
What are you thinking! Beer, of course! You can buy it in most stadiums and whatever you can fit in your flask that will get past stadium security.

For up to 8 guests

The watchword here is portability. Normally we would never advocate such a high-fat, free-radical-filled meal—think of your complex-

ion—but it is football, and you should never fight your theme. Aside from the beer brats, you can pick up most of your menu on the way to the game.

Beer Brats

Should you hail from the state of Wisconsin, your faithful founders realize that you already have a beer brat recipe that has been in your family for several generations so skip this section and just make them the way you were taught. For the rest of us, we'll start by pointing out that you don't actually boil the beer brats, you only simmer them. Boiling would rupture the casing and then they won't look pretty.

Two 12-ounce cans or bottles beer
   (for the brats)
12 bratwurst sausages
1 sweet onion, chopped
12 bratwurst buns
One 16-ounce jar spicy mustard (see Note for
   more information)

Begin by pouring two cans of beer, cheap and domestic works just fine, into a large pot. Add the brats and chopped onion. Add water to the beer to provide enough liquid to simmer the brats. Again, you don't actually want to boil them. Just heat the water-beer solution on medium heat until steam is rising from the surface, but the liquid isn't bubbling. Simmer for 15 to 20 minutes, remove the pot from the heat. Pour this liquid and the brats into a container that has a lid. After you let the brats and liquid cool, put the lid on and slide it in the fridge overnight.

Once you get to the stadium, heat your portable grill for about 20 minutes or until you can put your hand, palm down, 2 inches above the grate for 4 to 5 seconds. Add the brats. Use tongs to turn the brats every few minutes so they are a nice golden brown. This will only take about 15 minutes since you've simmered the brats beforehand. Serve the brats on a bun with the spicy mustard. Everything else is pretty easy.

Note: Morgan prefers Cleveland Stadium brand.

Chips/Pretzels

Two 11.5-ounce bags potato chips/pretzels

Put your chips/pretzels in large, brightly colored plastic bowls—you may be tailgating, but that's no excuse to live like a savage and eat out of the bag—horses do that! We'll let you convert two points on that TD if you have team logo bowls or bowls in team colors.

Precut Veggie Sticks and Dip

Two 8-ounce bags precut vegetables
One 8-ounce container vegetable dip

Put the veggie sticks on a platter and the dip in a bowl. Serve on either your tailgate or a small portable table.

S'mores

S'mores are lot more fun when you are cooking them over an open flame, as it ceases to be cooking and transforms into a social activity. But if you are tailgating at home and serving your S'mores at the start of the second half this really isn't practical. You'll need twelve to fifteen wooden skewers, if you are making the S'mores over a grill. If you're making them in the oven, use aluminum foil. While heating the marshmallows over a candle in your living room might seem like a good idea after you've had one six-pack, we really don't recommend it as your carpet or new leather sofa could be in serious jeopardy.

One 16-ounce box graham crackers
Two 6-ounce Hershey chocolate bars, broken
into blocks, 2 blocks per S'more
One 16-ounce bag marshmallows

Preheat the oven to 350 degrees. To assemble the individual S'mores, break a large graham cracker in half, sandwich in two blocks of the chocolate bar and a marshmallow, then wrap in foil, and bake in the preheated oven. Bake for 10 minutes.

Your portable grilling method of choice will dictate the onsite method employed for making S'mores. Should your tailgate involve a charcoal grill, your *rush* party will be able to roast their marshmallows over the open flames. Once warmed, melted, or charred to taste, the marshmallow and two blocks of chocolate are then sandwiched between the graham cracker halves. However, if your tailgate relies on a portable gas grill, the S'mores will need to be assembled, wrapped in aluminum foil, and then warmed on the grill for about ten minutes. Prepare them immediately after removing the brats from the grill, but leave them wrapped in the foil until your *rushees* are ready to consume them.

enjoys doing this little dance while singing "Hail to the Redskins" every time they score, but also because she wants to keep the party atmosphere as lively as the gridiron. If you have fans rooting, not only for the team, but also against each other, you keep everyone interested in the game (even if it's a rout, and that's a lot more fun).

In some parts of the country, football is revered in a fervor similar to religion. If this is the case for your community, your tailgate party must absolutely incorporate local traditions as well as a few of your own special touches. It's also important to be aware of any team traditions, songs, and fan rituals.

For example, when Morgan lived in Tampa, she learned never to attend a Buccaneers game without her Pirate flag and the ever-so-important beads. She also learned to embrace the trademark "Tampa!" "Bay!" cheer. If you are confused about what your team's traditions are, just call that cute guy you met at he sports bar last week.

MAKE THE MOOD COME ALIVE

Party Math: Game + Guests = atmosphere.

Although Brooksie is a devout Redskins fan, she always invites a couple of people who like the other team. Why? Mainly because she really

TAKE YOUR PARTY FROM GREAT TO FIRST RATE (OR HOW WE DID IT)

If you are at home, have all your TVs on, providing multiple watching options. Should children be in attendance, give them their own TV and viewing area. This keeps them separate from that single guy who hasn't learned to tone down, "Run you motherf*****, run!" Also if you are at home, visit your local sporting goods store and pick up a few hats that you can scatter on the food table. Later, you can raffle them off as fabulous prizes.

At the stadium, don't forget to pack your red-and-white-checked tablecloth from the Kentucky Derby party to spread out over a collapsible table or the actual tailgate if possible. And since you're bringing a table, bring chairs too. Folding patio or beach chairs allow your group to stake out its tailgating space.

Team flags. You have to put them on the car, you really do. It will allow you to experience an esprit de corps with your fellow fans as you drive to the game and tailgate.

Bring a portable radio and listen to the local pregame show. Why should you miss out on this bonus football coverage just because you are at the stadium? Plus it's not a good idea to run down your car battery.

A tip for the single girls—buy more food than your party really needs—you can offer something to the cute guys next to you grilling

those sad little hotdogs. The magical combination of beer brats and a girl who knows her football will wow any red-blooded American male.

TIMELINE

Organizing your tailgate begins with a location decision and ticket availability. If your *rush group* is composed of season ticket holders to your alma mater, all you need to do is pick the game and put the word out via e-mail. If you need to buy tickets, get hard confirmation of attendance from your fellow tailgaters at least a month in advance.[3] This should be done through either personal telephone calls or personal e-mail.

Tailgating in your party space requires far less coordination. Simply e-mail your "A list" guests two weeks prior to the game you've selected. Note that both the first game of the season and major rivalries tend to draw interest from even less avid fans.

One week before the tailgate—As we mentioned before, we have it on good authority that there is nothing sexier than a woman who knows her game. Brush up on your team's

---

3. In an organized event such as this, hard confirmation should be defined as a check or cash to purchase said invitee's ticket.

stats, personnel changes, and pertinent info by devoting 15 minutes a day to the sports page. You'll be able to spark conversation with statements like, "I'm so excited about Joe Gibbs's return to NFL coaching!" Inventory your team logo gear and determine if you need to borrow anything. You may find that last year's T-shirt or jersey doesn't look as flattering as you would like. If this is the case, you must definitely get a more attractive team-supporting outfit.

The night before the tailgate—Pick up your menu items from the grocery store. Simmer the brats in beer. If you are tailgating at the stadium, clean out your car. If you are tailgating in your home, tidy up your party space.

The day of the tailgate—If you are tailgating at the stadium, your caravan will need to leave several hours before kickoff. Determine how long it will take you to drive to the stadium and park, plus a minimum of two hours to tailgate. Now do the math backward—this is when you need to leave. Once you arrive, heat the grill, start cooking the Beer Brats, snacking, and drinking beer.

Twenty minutes before kickoff—start the S'mores, chug your last beer, and when the S'mores are eaten, head to the gates.

If you are tailgating in your home, the tailgate should start about one hour prior to kickoff so your guests can enjoy the pregame show and get excited about the big game.

Thirty minutes before your guests arrive— Set out any fan paraphernalia you might have, i.e., your decorations. Assemble the S'mores. Set out the chips and veggies on your food table or simply use the coffee table to eliminate time away from the television.

Once your guests start to arrive—Grill the Beer Brats.

Halftime—Bake the S'mores and serve.

A WORD ABOUT . . . FOOTBALL

As we've alluded to above, enjoying football has very little to do with years of researching the rules, regulations, and rivalries. Football and tailgating have become social experiences accessible and fun to a variety of people regardless of their actual interest in the game. While knowing the rules and the "ins" and "outs" of your team is a great conversation starter and a way to instantly win the respect of your fellow fans, even a gal who doesn't know pass interference from offside can enjoy football and this party.

Don't root for the team with the prettiest colors or the one that you think is most likely to win. You need to understand that your team is the team of geography, not the team of destiny. So just because the home team was 1–15 in the sixteen-game season doesn't mean you can trade them in for the defending Super Bowl champs. Crying in your beer can be just as much fun as toasting a victory.

Frankly, this party is no different than any other party. It comes down to the same three elements: good food (and drinks), good fun, and good friends. While Brooksie is a dedicated football fan, Morgan has no idea what a tailback does. She does, however, look forward to football season every year for the lazy Sunday afternoons spent with friends drinking beer, having some pork of various description, and indulging in lively halftime conversation. Football is also an opportunity to engage in civic pride and learn more about the people in the community that you call home. Don't let all the strategy of some silly little game get in the way of your good time and rob you of an afternoon with your friends.

ITALIAN STREET FESTIVAL

Vino, vidi, vici
(Wine, I saw, I conquered)

CONCEPT

Morgan pays tribute to the Murray Hill neighborhood in Cleveland. During her vaguely misspent youth, Morgan enjoyed many a late summer night taking in an authentic Italian-American street festival. Now, RSG offers you this party-style rendition.

In religious tradition, the Feast of the Assumption is the major festival celebrating Mary. Traditionally, it is marked on August 15. On and around that date, in many cities there is a street fair with rides, games, snow cones, and Italian food. In short, the works. Rather than attending a fair with a bunch of people you don't know, re-create the feeling of the street fair with dinner and games in your home. This is not the Feast of the Assumption per se, it's more an Indian Summer fair with Italian elements perfect for the middle or the end of September.

Your colors are red, white, and green. Begin at the center of it all—your food table. The trusty red-and-white-checked tablecloth returns and is home to some Chianti wine bottles in baskets.

DECORATIONS

1 red-and-white-checked vinyl tablecloth, the dimension of your food table

4 Chianti bottles with basket bottoms

1 keg of red curling ribbon

1 keg of green curling ribbon

4 strands of white Christmas lights per 1,500 square feet of party space

1 package of 30 white tea lights per 1,500 square feet of party space

4 medium-height white candle tapers

24 helium balloons in red, white, and green—about 8 of each color

30 red, green, or white paper or plastic plates

40 red, green, or white napkins

30 sets of plastic cutlery

40 red, green, or white plastic cups

Carnival game items—see "Make the Mood Come Alive" to select your games and supplies

Thumbtacks

Various Fellini films

Give your party space the curling ribbon treatment. What carnival is complete without the confetti? The more the merrier. So get to it, this could take a little time. If you're confused, refer back to New Martini's Eve, for appropriate curling ribbon decor practice. You still have one more quiz to pass before bids are handed out.

Lighting, lighting, lighting. This time, start with the stars, and use your white Christmas tree lights and thumbtacks to string the lights across the ceiling, looping down from the ceiling, to create an urban carnival atmosphere. Let's talk, eye level. Use your white tea lights to bring more light at eye level on the bookshelves, coffee table, on top of the TV—wherever. Remember, you are relying on those Christmas tree lights and these tea lights to wrap you in the warmth of a Tuscan sunset. Candles. Insert the white tapers into your empty Chianti bottles restaurant-style. If they fit securely, light them, otherwise just rely on the look. Scatter them on your food table and anyplace that needs an authentic touch.

Now we are going somewhere we haven't taken you before. You'll have to make a trip to a store that sells helium balloons—come on, that's most grocery stores these days. Purchase two dozen red, white, and green balloons to sell the fantasy and soften the corners of your room.

FOOD

Carry forward the theme of Italian culture with your food selection. But don't bore your guests with pasta and red sauce. Serve Shallot Pesto Pasta and honor street-fair culture with Snow Cones. Well, Snow Cones for Adults: Frozen Strawberry Daiquiris.

MENU

Shallot Pesto Pasta
Tomato and Fresh Mozzarella Salad
Snow Cones for Adults (aka Frozen
Strawberry Daiquiris)

For up to 20 guests

Shallot Pesto Pasta

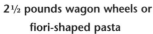

2½ pounds wagon wheels or
    fiori-shaped pasta
5 pounds boneless, skinless chicken breasts
Olive oil–flavored cooking spray
Salt
Crushed red pepper flakes to taste (optional)
¾ cup plus 2 tablespoons coarsely chopped fresh
    shallots

80 medium-size fresh basil leaves, torn into
    pieces, plus ¾ cup chopped fresh basil or
    ¾ cup prepackaged fresh basil
7 tablespoons chopped garlic (Polaner or other
    brand, chopped and packaged)
1 cup olive oil
¾ cup plus 2 tablespoons water
¾ cup plus 2 tablespoons dry white wine or
    white cooking wine
3½ tablespoons ground pepper
2½ pounds frozen asparagus spears

In a large cooking pot pour sufficient water to cover 2½ pounds of pasta. Bring to a boil and cook until al dente, about 8 to 10 minutes. Drain the pasta and let it cool. Cut the boneless, skinless chicken breasts into ¼-inch cubes. Spray a large sauté pan with olive-oil–flavored cooking spray and cook over medium-high heat. Salt lightly. Add crushed red pepper flakes to taste, if desired. Set the chicken aside to cool. Combine the chopped shallots with the fresh basil, garlic, olive oil, water, white wine, and black pepper in a food processor. Liquefy.

Steam the asparagus spears. When the asparagus is tender, drain and spray the spears lightly with the olive oil cooking spray and salt lightly. After the asparagus has cooled, cut the spears into ¼-inch sections. Combine in the pasta pot with the cooled, drained pasta, chicken, and asparagus. Pour in the shallot sauce and stir well. Use a spatula to remove all the sauce from the sides of the food processor. Finally, add the prepackaged, prechopped basil. Stir well and serve in a large serving bowl.

Tomato and Fresh Mozzarella Salad

2 large fresh tomatoes
1 pound round mozzarella
Dried oregano (optional)
2 tablespoons prepackaged Polaner chopped
**   basil packed in olive oil**

This isn't hard. Slice the tomatoes into rounds and place on a decorative plate alternating with round slices of mozzarella. If you are a fancy type, sprinkle lightly with dried oregano and basil.

Snow Cones for Adults
(aka Frozen Strawberry Daiquiris)

Everyone loves a daiquiri. As in just one. But that's because most daiquiri mixes are way too sweet. But since your party highlights a signature cocktail, it's important that people try it, like it, and ask for a second. So we've come up with a recipe that won't make your guests feel like the drink is coated with sugar but it will still evoke great carnival snow-cone memories.

Two 8-pound bags ice
Six 16-ounce bags frozen strawberries,
**   slightly thawed**
30 ounces sweetened lime juice
4 liters light, white rum

It's really only possible to make about five drinks per standard, 40-ounce blender. You may want to consider borrowing an extra blender from a friend to make drinks faster. Fill approximately half the blender with ice. Add 1 cup of the slightly thawed strawberries, 2½ ounces of the sweetened lime juice, and 10 ounces of light white rum. Put the lid back on the blender and hit the mix button. Blend thoroughly, so there are no chunks of ice. Repeat as needed.

MAKE THE MOOD COME ALIVE

Do you have an Italian granny? If you do, we suggest you raid her record collection. No Italian granny? You need your Sinatra and your Dean Martin, think New York in the 1950s—ask yourself, "What would Sophia Loren listen to?"

Despite your festive lighting scheme and Italian-restaurant-quality food table, the decorations are a bit sparse. But that's why you'll offer Fellini films and carnival games. A little weird avant-garde cinema will catch your guests' attention, but not distract them to the point where conversation withers. And besides, you've got games to play.

The dartboard returns from the St. Patrick's Day Pub Party, but with balloons. Suddenly, it's that cheesy game where you pop the balloon.

Take aim in another direction. Set up some empty wine bottles and see if any of the guests can toss a rubber ring around the neck of the bottle.[4]

And our favorite carnival game—tossing Ping-Pong balls into goldfish bowls. However, if your friends are members of PETA, you might want to find another game. This is cheap as hell and can be a true test of motor skills after that third daiquiri. It's best to set this up in the kitchen or bathtub. You'll need three somewhat large clear glass containers and three goldfish. We like using flower vases, oversized margarita glasses, and if you are really trendy—goldfish bowls. See if your guests can toss that Ping-Pong ball into the container and win the goldfish. What they do with the fish is up to them.

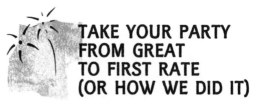

TAKE YOUR PARTY FROM GREAT TO FIRST RATE (OR HOW WE DID IT)

Find authentic carnival posters—we'll even settle for advertisements on paper in Italian—and hang them in your less decorated party spaces. Always remember Morgan's and Brooksie's watchwords—hallways and bathrooms.

The bocce ball tournament. No one under sixty really knows how to play bocce ball, so you can pretty much make up your own rules and set this up wherever you want, preferably outside. Do not attempt if your outside party space is a high-rise terrace, for tragedy could ensue.

Add gelato to the menu. Häagen-Dazs makes an excellent grocery store gelato. If you live in the mid-Atlantic and can get to a branch of Vaccaro's, do so, immediately.[5]

TIMELINE

This is a relaxing, fun party that will lift your spirits as you say farewell to summer. Send out the e-mail after Labor Day.

---

4. An unused, new, fresh, pet toy makes an excellent rubber ring. Fluffy deserves her toys too, and she can have this one after the party.
5. Vaccaro's has a lovely Web site, so there's no reason you can't have goodies delivered to your door.

Two weeks before the party—Inventory the decorations. Decide which carnival games your party will include.

One week before the party—With the seasons changing, it's probably a good time to consult your hairstylist for a color fit for fall. Purchase any decorations you will need and supplies for the carnival games. Borrow, beg, or steal the music for the party.

The evening before the party—Do your grocery shopping. Rent the Fellini films. Tidy up your party space.

The morning of the party—Getting the carnival lights up can be a little tricky. Give yourself plenty of time and start early. The same goes for the curling ribbon treatment. Once you're done, make the liquor store run and pick up the balloons. Now you'll have most of the day to work out, nap, and make yourself sparkle on the outside.

4 P.M.	Set up the carnival games and arrange the balloons.
4:45 P.M.	Cube the chicken.
5 P.M.	Put the water on to boil for the pasta. Add pasta when it boils. Cook until tender.

5:30 P.M.	Chop the shallots and make the sauce; steam your asparagus; sauté the chicken. Cut asparagus into sections.
5:45 P.M.	Make the Tomato and Fresh Mozzarella Salad. Mix together Shallot Pesto Pasta with chicken.
5:55 P.M.	Light the candles, turn on your carnival lights, and start that Fellini film.
6 P.M.	Make the first pitcher of daiquiris as your guests arrive.

A WORD ABOUT . . . CELEBRATING YOU

Parties should always reflect their hostess. In this party, Morgan shares many fond childhood memories, as well as her husband's Italian-American heritage. The combination creates not only a fun atmosphere, but it's easy because the intimate knowledge of the mood and look can be created without much thought.

So let's talk about you, *rushee*. What are you celebrating about yourself? Have you recently moved to a new area of the country and because of that will miss a local festival or event that you would like to share with people you've met recently? Re-create it in your home and invite your new friends over. Do you have a cultural tradition that is different or fun? Share it! Is there a special memory that always makes you smile? How can you turn it into a party theme? Do you make a killer quiche or are you a world champion bowler? Let your party highlight those skills.

When you share yourself with your guests, they will feel closer to you and friendships will be strengthened. It will also remind them that everyone is worth celebrating and hopefully spark their creative party-hosting instincts. Once you've trained your *rush group* in this crucial party method, you'll no longer be the only one hosting the great parties. Plus, the nights spent suffering through those boring restaurant birthday dinners will be over. Isn't that alone worth training your friends?

DON'T BE BEIGE

A RANT BY BROOKSIE

Often, when I meet someone for the first time, I'll describe him or her as a color. I happen to be "fuchsia"—outgoing, not afraid to accept a dare, I frequently have trouble differentiating my outside voice from my inside voice, thus giving the appearance of being very opinionated. Morgan is an "electric blue"—also outgoing and always ready for a good time, but she has an uncanny ability to smile and nod in a friendly sort of manner, all while planning your death.

When figuring our guest lists, we do our best to focus on the rainbow—bright, vibrant personalities that will provide great conversation and keep a party moving through their participation in party activities. However, we frequently find ourselves being forced to invite someone's girlfriend, boyfriend, or roommate, who is, well, "beige."

"Beige" is synonymous with boring. "Beige" people speak only when spoken to and even then, they frequently respond only in yes or no form. "Beige" is worse than "gray"—might be interesting if they weren't always talking about killing themselves—and "taupe"—used to be fun before they gave up drugs, alcohol, fun, had two kids, etc. Even "ecru" is better than "beige" because "ecru" people are at least passionate about something; granted, it's probably bugs or coins or something you'd never want to get stuck talking about, but at least they will talk about something.

Bottom line, "beige" people are never going to be at the top of the invite list, unless all your friends are "beige," but "beige" people aren't really big party givers, so the point is moot. So, if you have a sneaking suspicion that you might be "beige," these tips are for you.

Never use plain old "yes" or "no" to respond to questions in a social setting. A conversation involves two people exchanging views and opinions. One person asking questions and another person responding "yes" or "no" is an inquisition.

If you are uncomfortable answering questions, ask someone an open-ended question like "How was your vacation in Aruba?" Then listen. Intently. While the other person may not learn much about you, that individual will think you were really interested in him or her. And then seal the deal for a move up to "cream" by paying them a nice compliment—"You look so great, have you been losing weight?"

Smile when you talk to people. Even if you are boring, smiling will at least make you appear friendly. And if you are shy, smiling a lot will make people think you are flirting. Either way, you're bound to move up to a nice pastel.

Join us in the world of popular culture. Read a book your friends have been talking about. Start watching *Queer Eye for the Straight Guy* or at the very least, *American Idol*. See a movie or two. Glance over a newspaper or, like Morgan, develop a glossy magazine habit. Stuff is going on in the world, and you might even find some of it interesting. Have trouble forming an opinion of your own on it? Steal someone else's. Just replace three stars with "I thought it was a sophisticated story, but it could've been better told."

Stop obsessing about what other people might think about you and embrace your true color. If you think you're "beige," they know you're "beige," and that's one of the worst opinions they can form about you. You can only surprise them with your incredible singing voice at karaoke, your ability to tie the stem of a cherry in your mouth, or that ingenious plan to establish a lasting peace in the Middle East. While they may act shocked, it's because they have suddenly realized that you were never really "beige" at all, and they are probably thinking of questions to ask you.

Chapter Eight

OCTOBER

COLUMBUS DAY PARTY

Or, how to turn any old day into an excuse to celebrate!

CONCEPT

Actual holidays can be so confining to your creativity as they come with prepackaged foods, colors, and traditions. We say, why wait for an actual holiday when you can hijack a bank and federal-employee holiday and make it your own? So, this party is for you! We offer some suggestions, based on our personal taste and prior party experiences, but use your imagination and start your own party tradition. Embrace it—this is your chance to become legendary!

Why Columbus Day? Columbus Day is one of the few federal holidays that has no real underlying tradition attached to it, aside from Native Americans protesting it and Italian Americans celebrating it at the Knights of Columbus Hall. In truth, Arbor Day would've done just as well. Please note we do not advocate this for more serious holidays like Veterans' Day or Martin Luther King Day. Besides, with Halloween at the end of October, having this party at the beginning of the month provides for nice spacing.

Since you will be trailblazing a new party concept we suggest limiting this event to no more than nine of your closest and most adventure-some friends. If many of your guests will have Columbus Day off from work, consider hosting this party on Sunday night. There's something more exciting about staying out late and playing on a Sunday night, when you know you don't have to go to work the next day. Plus, until HBO starts the new season of the *Sopranos*, no one has any plans on Sunday night anyway.

Just because the holiday is not real does not mean your decorations shouldn't be excessive. In order to achieve excess without budget distress, we suggest you hit the discount party store and buy whatever is on the markdown table. You may be mixing some Fourth of July stuff with Hawaiian luau party stuff, but that's O.K. because the traditional decorations for Columbus Day celebrate our rich cultural heritage, or at least that's what you should tell people when they ask why your centerpiece is a paper wedding bell. You should also consider this as an opportunity to buy your decorations for next year or recycle any random leftovers. The key word here is variety. You need to mix at least four different party themes. You know how we told you combining party themes was

DECORATIONS

Columbus Day banner
Party store salvage
Random assortment of 15 paper or plastic plates
Random assortment of 20 napkins
15 sets cutlery for all your guests; feel free to mix and match
Random assortment of 20 plastic cups

the equivalent of a rummage sale? Your goal here is to achieve that thematic cacophony. Remember the theme is there is no theme, because you're making this stuff up, and because guests will believe you when you explain, "But these are the traditional Columbus Day decorations" if you say it with sincerity and great pride. And if your guests still don't get it, point them to a banner that says "Happy Columbus Day."[1]

---

1. Remember the words in the RSG crest! *"Recycalada"* and *"attitudium."*

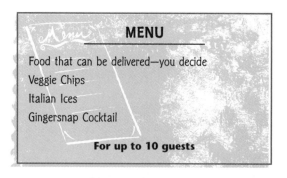

MENU

Food that can be delivered—you decide

Veggie Chips

Italian Ices

Gingersnap Cocktail

For up to 10 guests

Why, it's the "traditional" Columbus Day menu! To carry off the joke, it's important to present everything as a mythical tradition that you and your guests can winkingly share.

Nothing says Columbus Day like a visit from the Domino's guy! So order pizza for your guests. You may also want to pick up a few bags of Veggie Chips, and for dessert, present a selection of Italian ices. This is very traditional Columbus Day fare, and if anyone asks why, just tell them you are celebrating the bounty and diversity of America, where having food delivered to your home is a God-given right. Seriously, it's the Twelfth Amendment to the Constitution or something.

Gingersnap Cocktail

The traditional Columbus Day signature cocktail is the gingersnap. We believe strongly that the members of the Society of Recovering

Sorority Girls should be well read. Reading opens one up to new ideas and continues one's education. Glossy magazines focusing on travel, fashion, and celebrity dating are especially useful for broadening one's mind and making the individual well rounded. For example, the vodka advertisements in the August 2003 edition of *Travel & Leisure* magazine inspired us to take on this yummy and oh-so-traditional Columbus Day cocktail.

One 2-liter bottle of ginger ale
Two 1-liter bottles of Stoli Vanil vodka

Although originally prepared with Absolut Vanilla, we have a soft spot for the Stoli variety. Simply mix equal parts ice-cold ginger ale and Stoli Vanil vodka. Pour into a cocktail glass with ice. It's damn near as tasty as a Slurpee, but clearly for adults—something Starbucks would serve if only they had a liquor license.

MAKING THE MOOD COME ALIVE

Traditional Columbus Day celebrations and games are required! The traditional Columbus Day outfit is casual—jeans and a sweatshirt with your college logo (or you can substitute the logo of the college you wish you went to). You must also play traditional Columbus Day games, such as Trivial Pursuit, Cranium, Pictionary, Twister, Charades, Scategories, etc. However, under no circumstances is Jenga to be played—it's not a traditional Columbus Day game.

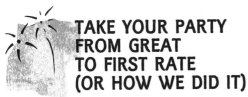

TAKE YOUR PARTY FROM GREAT TO FIRST RATE (OR HOW WE DID IT)

Offer fabulous prizes for your game winners. Of course, they must be traditional Columbus Day prizes. Rice-A-Roni and Turtle Wax work very nicely. If they offered it as a parting gift in the game shows of your youth, it's traditional Columbus Day.

Upgrade the quality of your delivered fare. Ditch the pizza and opt for Thai.

Add crepe paper streamers and balloons to your decorations. Nothing says traditional Columbus Day (or a child's birthday party) like crepe paper streamers and balloons.

TIMELINE

Two weeks before the party—Send out the e-mail invitation.

One week before the party—Determine which decorations you will recycle, and hit the discount party store sale table. Go to the liquor store and the grocery. Treat yourself to a relaxing massage at your local day spa. The stress release will make you glow from the inside out, all week.

The morning of the party—Tidy up the party space.

One hour before the party—Arrange the decorations chaotically. Pull out the takeout menus and place them on the coffee table along with the Veggie Chips. Remove board games from closets (but not Jenga, never Jenga).

45 minutes before the party—Return to your hair and makeup. Once the first guest arrives, call the takeout service and order the food. Make the first batch of gingersnaps.

A WORD ABOUT . . . CELEBRATION

People often forget that life is to be enjoyed, and a hearty sense of humor is one of the best assets you can have. We provided this party to prove that you don't have to wait for a special event to celebrate. You can celebrate for the sake of celebrating. We host parties because we legitimately enjoy people (well, some people), to make memories, and deepen bonds with friends. In response, our friends eagerly await our next event and have also started to plan events of their own. This creates a more active and vibrant social life for everyone. And with the pressures of work, relationships, and bill paying, who doesn't need a safe space with friends to cut loose?

Additionally, this party demonstrates something we believe in very strongly—entertaining isn't hard. The elements from this party are drawn mainly from games and takeout menus we have. Hosting a party doesn't have to be a big production that takes weeks to plan. If you focus on the fact that parties are meant to be a time to share, and not just another stressor in your already busy life, you can get over the fact that you just bought a premade dessert at the store two hours before your guests arrived, instead of making it yourself. So get down off that cross and shake off the party obligations your mother and grandmother beat into you. You can party like a rock star even when you are the hostess.

HALLOWEEN PARTY II

All treats, no tricks, no kids

CONCEPT

Just because you've outgrown trick or treating doesn't mean you've outgrown Halloween. Donning a costume and parading throughout the city is still fun, if not more fun, than when you were a kid. In general, the parties are bigger, better, and lack adult supervision. Yours will be no exception. This party is about creating a frighteningly good time for your grown-up friends.

Halloween, as we think of it today, is a mixture of the Celtic New Year festival, the Roman Pomona Day, and the Catholic Church's All Saints' Day. But even after centuries of celebrations, this holiday continues to evolve. Sadly, because some cults have chosen Halloween as their special holiday, the event now has a slightly tarnished reputation. And so, it is the task of the Society of Recovering Sorority Girls to return Halloween to its rightful place in American history by hosting Halloween parties that celebrate its eclectic combination of Celtic, Roman, and Catholic traditions.

Costume? Did you really have to ask? Of course you'll be insisting your guests wear costumes, and you have to wear one as well. If

DECORATIONS

1 fog machine

One 1-quart bottle fog machine liquid

4 sheets of poster board

Two 3-ounce bottles of gray craft paint

1 medium point paintbrush

1 utility knife

1 black Magic Marker

3 strands of white Christmas tree lights per
    1,500 square feet of party space

Thumbtacks

12 white tea lights or assorted Halloween
    candles

2 to 3 black lightbulbs

Two 1.4-ounce packages of cobwebs

3 pumpkins

3 votive candles

3 plastic pumpkins for candy

30 paper or plastic orange or black dessert plates

40 orange or black napkins

40 orange or black hot beverage cups

you're totally stumped for ideas, just look to the holiday's roots. Don a white sheet as a toga, place a wreath on your head, and call yourself the Roman Goddess Pomona—the goddess of fruits and gardens.

A fog machine might seem like an extreme investment for one party, but trust us—it's the hallmark decoration for this party. First, it's very impressive. Your guests will be referring to "the Halloween party with the fog machine" for months. But most important, a fog machine placed in an out-of-the-way corner of your party space allows you to transform any party space in an absolutely amazing, mysterious way.

Even you won't recognize your own home. Besides, it's only about $25 at the local craft store and offers a more impressive effect than dry ice without all the hassle.

Since your party space will be transformed into an eerie cemetery, you'll need to make some personalized tombstones. Cut the poster boards into rectangular halves so you can make a total of eight tombstones. Use a large serving bowl to trace a round shape around the top, and cut off the excess poster board with the utility knife. Paint the front of the poster board with the gray paint. After the paint dries, you'll need to decide what—note not who—has died and write that on the tombstone with the black Magic Marker. Here is where knowing your guests becomes important, as you will need to balance humor and celebration with the concept of death. These examples should clarify:

Our friend Tom had gotten married a few months before Halloween, so we made a tombstone that said, "R.I.P. Tom's Bachelor Days" with the date of the wedding. His new wife liked it.

Our friend Carla had just accepted a new job which was a prestigious step up from her old position as a staff assistant. Her tombstone read, "Deceased: Carla's Staff Ass Career." It's now hanging in Carla's basement.

And because Brooksie's birthday is the day before Halloween, she always makes a tombstone that reads, "Here Lies Brooksie's Youth" with the preceding day's date.

These tombstones should make people laugh, not feel like they've lost something.[2] Hang them at eye level along the walls of your main party space.

Lighting, or the lack of it, is key. Your white Christmas tree lights return, as do your tea lights. Securing with thumbtacks, hang your white Christmas tree lights along the walls of your party space, approximately 2 inches from the ceiling. You'll be creating a border of light around the perimeters of the party space and relying only on tea lights for the center sections of your room. Replace two or three of the lights in your party space with black lightbulbs. It'll make the fog even eerier.

Moving on to the cobwebs, two standard packages will help you cover nearly every corner of your party space. They should also hang off the white Christmas tree lights.

Your final decoration incorporates a tradition the Irish brought to the United States during the potato famine—jack-o'-lanterns. Carve those pumpkins in a creative fashion and insert the three votive candles to cast shadows. Place

MENU

Candy (lots of it)
Apple Slices with Caramel Dip
Banana Chips
Cajun-Spiced Popcorn
Mulled Wine Cider

For up to 20 guests

---

2. Additionally you can always incorporate the Catholic tradition of All Saints' Day by offering to pray for whatever they've lost so it can go to heaven.

them in your party space on coffee tables, end tables, and perhaps by the door.

Because this party starts at 9 P.M., your guests shouldn't expect a lot of food. This menu is designed to spark some of your childhood memories, while catering to your grown-up tastes. Banana Chips and Cajun-Spiced Popcorn fulfill the crunchy side of your junk food cravings. But it wouldn't be Halloween without a variety of sugary treats. So use your imagination when selecting candy, which will go on your food table and should be scattered around the party space in the plastic pumpkins. The Apple Slices with Caramel Dip pay homage to the Roman Goddess Pomona.

4 large bags assorted candy (trick-or-treat size bags range from 13.3 ounces to 32 ounces, depending on the type of candy)

6 apples

One 18-ounce package fat-free caramel dip

1 lemon

8 ounces banana chips

3 packages microwave popcorn

2 ounces Cajun-spice seasoning

1 case red or apple-spiced white wine

Several packages of mulling spices
(see Note for more information)

Cooking time is practically nonexistent. All you do is purchase the candy and banana chips, and dump their contents into the plastic pumpkins. Slice the apples, squirt with the juice of the lemon to keep them from going brown, and serve on a tray with the caramel dip. Make the microwave popcorn according to the directions, sprinkle with the Cajun seasoning, and that's it. Besides, you need more time to focus on your costume.

Prepare the mulled wine cider according to the directions given on the package of mulling spices. Warm in a Crock-Pot.

Note: Read the instructions on the packages of mulling spices. One we used required vermouth. Another added sugar water.

MAKE THE MOOD COME ALIVE

Your eerie lighting scheme and the fog machine offer as much atmosphere as any haunted house we've ever been too. Plus the lit candles take on a special meaning for this party. October 31 marked the end of sun season for the Druids, and after the crops were harvested and stored for the long winter, cooking fires in the homes would be extinguished. The Druids, the Celtic priests, would light fresh fires and offer sacrifices of crops and animals to prepare for the season of darkness. The next day, all families would receive embers from the new flames to reignite their cooking fires. But if this is too much for you to remember, just tell people you're trying to make it scary.

Remember when you were little and there was always that one family that went all out for Halloween and played the cassette tape of people screaming for trick-or-treaters? Yeah, that's weird. We don't recommend you do that. Instead, show classic horror movies like *Night of the Living Dead*, *Psycho*, and *Carrie* as the backdrop. Pretty much everyone has seen them, so you won't mind the fog obscuring most of the picture.

Prizes for creative costumes are a must! You're asking guests to participate in your theme—reward them for their efforts. Plus the costumes are the conversation starters, so it's very important to have solid guest buy-in.

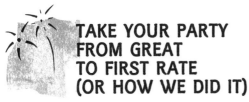

TAKE YOUR PARTY FROM GREAT TO FIRST RATE (OR HOW WE DID IT)

Instead of using white Christmas tree lights, opt for orange. They cast a very eerie glow over everything. Add a few pumpkin- or apple-

scented candles to provide the smell of the fall harvest.

Purchase a few disposable cameras and have your guests take lots of pictures. Have your favorite shot printed as postcards to be used as the invitations for next year's Halloween party.

Add glow-in-the dark skeletons to your decorations. You can hang them from the ceiling and off the Christmas tree lights. Now it's truly a dead man's party!

TIMELINE

Halloween is October 31, which isn't always an ideal party night. However, if you cannot hold your party on the night of Halloween, you must host it the weekend before. Do *not*, under any circumstances, try to hold this party the weekend after Halloween. No one will dress up, and standing around in a foggy living room will just seem odd. Also keep in mind Halloween is a major party night for adults in many metropolitan areas. If you'll have stiff competition, claim your date and start spreading the word in early October.

Three weeks before the party—Send your e-mail invitation.

Two weeks before the party—Inventory decorations. Start shopping the sales. Decide on a costume that works with your hairstyle and doesn't involve any weird face paint that could make you look hideous in pictures.

One week before the party—Cut and paint the tombstones. Finish purchasing the decorations.

The night before the party—Do your grocery shopping. Pick up the videos. Review your RSVP list and write epitaphs on the tombstones. Carve the jack-o'-lanterns.

The morning of the party—Tidy the party space. Begin decorating. Hanging the Christmas tree lights can be a bit tedious, so take your time and do a good job. Move on to the cobwebs. Once you've gotten all the hard work out of the way, reward yourself with a preparty nap.

5 P.M.	Finish decorating by hanging the tombstones, placing the jack-o'-lanterns on the tables and/or the front door, and putting the tea lights in the center sections of your party space.
6 P.M.	Eat some dinner. Your menu is light, so you'll need something a bit more substantial beforehand.
8 P.M.	Prepare and place the food on the table. Start the first batch of mulled wine.

8:30 P.M.	Put on your costume and replace 2 or 3 regular lightbulbs with black lights.
8:50 P.M.	Start the fog machine and the first horror movie. Light the votive candles in the jack-o'-lanterns and the tea lights.
9 P.M.	Greet your guests as they arrive and offer them candy.
11 P.M.	Give out awards for costumes.

 ## A WORD ABOUT . . . ENCOURAGING GOOD GUEST ETIQUETTE

Although the primary focus of this book is on the hostess, we must never forget about the guests. After all, your job as a hostess is to make your guests feel comfortable, entertained, wined, and dined. But that's not to say guests are completely off the hook. They are still very much as the word states, "guests." So how do you ensure they partake of your hospitality in the same loving manner it was envisioned, articulated, and hosted?

Start with clear communication. Your invitation should always state the time the party will begin, the address of your home, and driving instructions or a map, a method to RSVP, details as to what you are celebrating, and any other pertinent information. For example, if the party starts at an odd time, be sure to state what type of menu you'll be serving. People prepare differently for a cocktail party offering just appetizers than they would for a seven-course meal. Is there any special dress? Tell them! Do they need to bring something? Be specific about it.

Anticipate your guests' needs. Always, always, always be sure to have a fresh roll of toilet paper in your bathroom and additional rolls in sight. Have nonalcoholic beverages to offer designated drivers. If you don't permit smoking in your home and some of your guests smoke, set up a bucket or empty flower pot with sand on the balcony, patio, or on the front porch—otherwise you risk picking up nasty butts as part of your cleanup.

Be true to your word. Integrity is an important RSG value, and you must always strive to remain true to your theme. This means you can't cop out and wear jeans when you host a Cabin Fever Beach Party. If you wear jeans, and your guests show up in skorts, sarongs, and ugly Hawaiian shirts, they'll feel embarrassed, possibly confused, and most likely annoyed—with you. And if you offer fun, fabulous prizes, you'd

better give them out. Never deny your guests the joy of going home feeling like winners.

As you nurture and develop your inner hostessing abilities, you'll find your guests excited about parties that require a specific dress, interactive socializing, and games. In fact, you'll realize that you've become so cool, they'll do anything you tell them to do. The result—guests are ensured of a great time and the hostess knows her guests will enthusiastically participate in the party. It's this trust between the hostess and her guests that fosters good guest etiquette.

TOP TEN SIGNS OF A BAD PARTY

1. There are more children than adults in attendance.
2. Two words: Cheez Whiz.
3. The only single guy in the room who is not your ex bears a striking resemblance to "Fat Bastard" from the Austin Powers movies and he wants to tell you about his collection of bikini underwear.
4. Three people live in the house hosting the party and there are four people in attendance.
5. They're calling it a Mardi Gras Party, and all you got was this stupid mask. Hello? Beads? Hurricanes? Beignets? Perhaps some Cajun Zydeco? Theme, people, think theme!
6. Let's just say, it's all fun and games until someone starts crying.
7. The host tells you to keep it down because he doesn't want you to wake his mother.
8. Uncle Henry is bartending and instead of giving you the glass of white wine you requested, he winks and says he'll make something special for a pretty lady like you.
9. Spirited debate about the best commercially available teeth whitener is considered part of the entertainment.
10. It's been scheduled in the middle of football play-offs and the hostess won't let you watch the game.

TOP TEN SIGNS OF A GOOD PARTY

1. The room is abuzz with conversations.
2. There's a theme with coordinating food and decorations.
3. The activities are so much fun there is 100 percent guest participation.
4. Nothing feels like it is missing.
5. Even though you only know a few people, you end up talking to everyone.
6. The guests are asking the host for one of the recipes.
7. Party favors!
8. The hostess has taken into account the needs of *each* guest when setting up the menu and activities. Did you invite your vegetarian friend to a plated-dinner pig roast? Shame on you!
9. The organized hostess is free to party with her party.
10. People are already using the phrase "When you host this party again next year" in their sentences.

Chapter Nine

NOVEMBER

BEAUJOLAIS NOUVEAU EST ARRIVÉ

Only one good thing ever came out of France: the wine!

CONCEPT

Just because you used to serve wine from a box or a resealable carafe, doesn't mean that you can't co-opt a great French wine marketing tradition. This is a sophisticated gathering of twelve friends with an emphasis on food, wine, and conversation.

Normally, your faithful founders avoid red wine. Brooksie thinks it tastes like bark, and Morgan believes that too much of it will stain your teeth. Additionally, wine selection can be an intimidating task for a busy hostess. Very few people have the time it takes to research wine and food pairings. In the past, people rigidly applied these so-called wine rules to the selection process. Missteps were horribly embarrassing. Today, home entertaining is a lot more fluid and places greater emphasis on personal taste and preferences rather than sommelier-quality savoir faire.

Recently American yuppies discovered that their local wine store would celebrate the arrival of the New Year's vintage of French Beaujolais starting on the third Thursday of November. In some cities, notably Detroit, this has become a popular event and celebration. This party is simplicity itself, because you only need one kind of wine: Beaujolais nouveau.

Each guest in your *rush group* will receive a handwritten invitation instructing him or her

DECORATIONS

12 plain ecru blank invitation cards with envelopes
1 grape bunch craft stamp
One 3-ounce bottle of Bordeaux craft paint
One 3-ounce bottle of green craft paint
1 paintbrush
20 ecru, gold, or cobalt blue tea lights
One 200-light strand of white Christmas tree lights per guest bathroom
6 feet of artificial or silk grape vine for each guest bathroom
12 plain ecru blank place cards
12 fondue dippers
2 standard fondue pots (ceramic preferred)
12 dessert plates (use your china if you have it)
24 napkins, cloth preferred, but heavy paper napkins are acceptable
12 balloon (red wine) wineglasses

to report to the local wine store and procure a bottle of Beaujolais nouveau to bring to the fabulous tasting party to be held at your home.

The focus is on the wine and casual elegance. Further, as you are going to be sending physical invitations to set the mood, let's not stretch that budget even farther.

The invitation is really the beginning of the party, and your first and best chance to set the mood. Paint your grape bunch stamp with the Bordeaux and green craft paint, and then stamp the front of your ecru cards. It should create a lovely, yet handmade look. On the inside, write the who, what, when, where, and why details, as well as the all-important RSVP deadline. An empty chair will look funny at this party. In addition, help your guests find the appropriate wine. In our invitations, we included a list of vintners who produce Beaujolais wine. Be sure to mail your invitations at least three weeks before your party. The party itself will be the first Saturday after the third Thursday in November.

As you've probably already guessed, lighting is crucial. An assortment of tea lights should adorn side tables and shelves. This time, your white Christmas tree lights are attached decoratively to the ceiling of your bathroom(s) to create a Beaujolais under the stars effect. Six feet of artificial or silk grape vine should be used around the mirror of each guest bathroom to finish this effect.

Let's talk people and seating. For this event to work do not invite more guests than you have seating. The mood is intimate, the conversation is crucial, and the food is fondue. All of these things make it undesirable to have guests in separate parts of the home or unable to sit back, relax, and enjoy. So, this is an event for dining room tables and assigned seating. You'll use the ecru place cards, which match the invitation paper, to assign seating. It's also fun to place a fact about fondue and fondue traditions on each card as a conversation starter for guests. For example, did you know that when a female guest loses her dipper in the fondue, tradition says that she must kiss every man present? Could be fun, if you've paid proper attention to your guest list.

For dishes use the dessert plates from your everyday dishes or actual china, if available. If you have dinnerware that is a jewel tone such as cobalt, emerald, burgundy, or gold or has a jewel-tone accent, so much the better. Also, if you have cloth napkins, now is the perfect occasion to bring them out. A simple but elegantly set table is the centerpiece of your party, as your guests will be sitting around it for most of the evening. The fondue pots will take up much of the room on the table and too much

decoration could create a fire hazard. The plates, the napkins, and the place cards are all that's necessary for a beautiful evening. Don't forget, you'll also need a wineglass for red wine for each guest.

MENU

Assorted Breads, Cheeses, and Grapes
Reduced-Fat Chocolate Dessert Fondue
Fresh Fruit, Ladyfinger Cookies, and Angel
Food Cake for Dipping

For up to 12 guests

This is a sophisticated late-evening party. As you are beginning after 9 P.M., there is no need for a full dinner and because the wine tasting is the main event, it is better not to have a full meal competing for your time, attention, and table space. Add French flair by incorporating French bread and a cheese and grape selection on trays for hors d'oeuvres. A fondue dessert course keeps your event European, but not completely French-themed. A tray of fresh fruit, ladyfinger cookies, and angel food cake served next to melting chocolate in the fondue pot makes an easy and satisfying dessert.

Ideally, this menu works best with at least

one fondue pot per six guests. If you can borrow one or even two fondue pots from a friend—do it. It will make your menu feel seamless, and it's less work for you during the actual party. Depending on the size of your table, additional fondue pots will make it easier for guests to dip their fondue items, keeping the focus on the wine, as opposed to the food. We'll also note conventional fondue wisdom states that chocolate should not be made in a stainless steel pot, more often used with broth or oil.

Assorted Breads, Cheeses, and Grapes

2 crusty French baguettes
1 pound assorted gourmet cheeses,
    especially Emmentaler
1 bunch seedless grapes

If you have a large silver platter or tray, now is the party to use it. If not, just repeat the layout that follows on two large dinner plates. Place the assorted cheeses in the center of the platter, tray, or plates. Next, divide the bunch of grapes into smaller bunches of four to five grapes. Place these smaller grape bunches around the cheeses. Create the final outer layer with the bread. Slice your crusty French baguettes into rounds and use them to line the outer edge of the platter, tray, or plates.

Reduced-Fat Chocolate Dessert Fondue

1 cup whipping cream
3 teaspoons cornstarch
1½ cups water
⅜ cup sugar
1½ teaspoons vanilla extract
⅜ cup unsweetened powdered cocoa
12 ounces Ghirardelli chocolate chips
2¼ teaspoons grated orange zest
4 tablespoons Grand Marnier

Combine the whipping cream, cornstarch, water, sugar, vanilla, and powdered cocoa in a pot on the stove. Heat on low heat, stirring frequently. As the ingredients combine, add the chocolate chips, orange zest, and Grand Marnier. Once the chocolate chips are dissolved, transfer the chocolate fondue to a fondue pot and serve.

Fresh Fruit, Ladyfinger Cookies, and Angel Food Cake for Dipping

1 angel food cake, cut into cubes
One 7-ounce package ladyfinger cookies
½ pound fresh strawberries
½ pound fresh kiwi slices (about 2 kiwis)
½ pound frozen blackberries, thawed

Slice the angel food cake into bite-size, fondue-dipping-appropriate cubes and place in a decorative bowl. Remove the ladyfinger cookies from their packaging, display—in a visually appealing design of your own imagination—on a salad or dinner plate. Clean but do not de-stem the strawberries. Place them in a bowl. Slice and peel the kiwis, serving them on a small plate. Drain the thawed blackberries from any juice in the bag, and place them in their own bowl. Serve these items, family-style, with the chocolate fondue. Since the fondue pots take up most of the table, it's best for you as the hostess to serve each item to your right and when it returns back to you, to place it in the kitchen, on a sideboard, or any location that isn't your dining table.

MAKE THE MOOD COME ALIVE

Nothing should compete with the sparkling conversation. The music should be classical and turned down low, so that while it is still audible, it's not overwhelming. If classical is too mellow for your crowd, consider some soft jazz and bonus points for French acid jazz. Under no circumstances, are you to play anything by Jordie, France's four-year-old rap phenomenon

from the early 1990s. Just because the French like it, doesn't automatically make it chic!

Since this is a wine-tasting event, you will want your guests to be able to record their thoughts and comments on the different bottles for future reference. We have provided wine-tasting terms for this purpose (see "A Word About . . ." at the end of this party). Now, when your faithful founders hosted this event, the wine definitions turned into a drinking game. Maybe it's because we just have rowdy friends.

The wine tasting makes your job as a hostess easier in a couple of different ways. First, you don't spend a lot of money on alcohol for the party. Second, you can always stimulate the conversation by bringing it back to the wine. "What bottle did you bring?" "Which Beaujolais should we try next?" "Have you ever been to the local vineyard?" When in doubt, return to the wine.

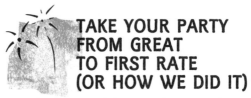

TAKE YOUR PARTY FROM GREAT TO FIRST RATE (OR HOW WE DID IT)

For glassware and the party favor, purchase enough red wineglasses to give to each guest. Paint a replica of the grape bunch pattern from the invitation onto the glass.

We also used postcards with Monet paintings to display the menu at each table. When combined with French poster art, the dining area was transformed into a French bistro.

Some old copies of *Wine Spectator* magazine supplemented the tasting terms. Brooksie also found a cute, French-themed notebook that became the evening's journal, documenting people's opinions on the wines, as well as pictures of the event.

Write the invitation text all in French. For example:

> *Vous êtes invité à une grande fête pour*
> *le Beaujolais nouveau!*
> Quand: le __ novembre, 21:00 heures
> Où: Chez (your name and address)
> RSVP avant que le __ novembre
> (one week before the party)

TIMELINE

This party requires more advanced preparation than any other party in this book. But don't worry, it's not much. Because you will be sending handwritten invitations, you need to provide yourself with enough snail-mailing time. So, make those invitations and get them in the mail no later than November 1. Members of

your *rush group* have time to receive the invitation, consider it, and *répondez s'il vous plaît* (respond) in time for you to shop, decorate, and find the perfect dressy casual outfit.

You are also very limited on dates for hosting this party. Beaujolais nouveau is released on the third Thursday of the month of November. It's best to host this party the Saturday evening immediately following the release. Anything later will conflict with Thanksgiving travel schedules.

Last week of October—Purchase craft store materials and make invitations.

November 1—Mail invitations.

Second week of November—Purchase wineglasses and glass paints. If you're painting the glasses, begin painting this week.

Third Thursday of November—Purchase your Beaujolais for the tasting. Make the place cards.

The morning of the party—Go to the grocery store.

7:30 P.M.	Decorate the bathroom and arrange the place cards.
8 P.M.	Finish getting ready.

8:30 P.M.	Arrange assorted cheeses on a tray and cut the bread; place the tray on a serving table. Wash the fruit, cut the angel food cake, and arrange them along with the cookies on a tray, but keep it in the kitchen until the fondue is served.
9 P.M.	Greet the *rush group* and start tasting the Beaujolais as soon as everyone has assembled.
10 P.M.	Begin preparing the fondue and serve when ready.

A WORD ABOUT . . . WINE TASTING

Some party mavens may try to confuse you by requiring you to acquire a professionally trained palate and learn a long list of fancy words that you can use to make other people feel intimidated. We say, drink more and talk less! How many ways do you need to learn to say, "Hmm, yummy" or "Eww, this tastes like bark." Sorority girls, by creed, are taught that honesty and integrity are two values that cannot be faked or compromised. Even when wine tasting, this still applies.

The object of the game is to have fun and to find something that suits your personal taste.

There is no need to engage in a battle of wits or terminology with your guests. That would be *un-Panhellenic!*

However, we have nothing against learning or self-improvement. Additionally, we realize that some members of your *rush group* may feel intimidated by the simple act of wine tasting itself, so here are a few simple wine-tasting terms you can use to put everyone at ease without compromising everything RSG stands for.

Acidic: A sharp, tart taste.

Aftertaste: Do we really need to tell you what that means?

Aromatic: A term used to describe the wine's bouquet or aroma.

Bitter: This describes a taste, not how you feel. Usually associated with younger wines, therefore a good term to remember when describing Beaujolais nouveau or how you feel about women younger than you.

Body: How the wine feels in the mouth. Light, medium, or full, depending on the wine's alcohol and extract.

Clean: A wine that doesn't taste funny.

Closed: Used to describe the taste of a wine that's been opened before its time. The flavor is somewhat incomplete.

Dry: A less sweet wine. Used to describe a lack of sugar, but not a lack of alcohol.

Fruity: Used to describe a flavorful bouquet of fully ripened grapes.

Legs: Ring around the collar for wine. The liquid residue left on the side of the glass, when tilted back and forth. Thicker, slower-moving legs denote higher alcohol content or residual sugar.

Musty: Wine that smells like Grandma's sweater drawer. Usually denotes dirty barrels.

Nose: A pretentious way to describe how the wine smells.

Soft: Much like cashmere, soft is always good. For wine it denotes a well-rounded flavor derived from mature tannins.

Tannic: A dry, astringent taste and mouth-feel from the skins, pits, and stalks.

CHRISTMAS CHAOS COVERED

The "Smart Girls Get Their Work Done So They Can Party" Party

CONCEPT

Just because you have to spend Thanksgiving Day with your family doesn't mean your whole weekend should be wasted. This party is strictly for the girls, so leave any boys or kids that you may have lying about at home. We should note this isn't a party per se, it's more like a celebration of *sisterhood* disguised as a holiday stress support group. Christmas Chaos Covered is about getting your work done so you can enjoy the holiday party schedule.

As we've explained, the party gods can be

cruel, and November begins the cruelest and most grueling of party seasons. But fear not, we've devised a way for you to keep having fun while you are dispatching your responsibilities. The watchword is *sisterhood*. When faithful *sisters* gather together to share their ideas, supplies, and a few cocktails, the benefits multiply. The labor is divided, the laughter cuts the stress, and everyone goes home with a sense of accomplishment. Not a bad deal for a Saturday afternoon.

In sorority life, most chapters hold weekly meetings called *chapter development*. It's up to the vice president to plan a nice mix of educa-

DECORATIONS

1 well-lit, decorated Christmas tree (What else are you going to do after you've eaten all that turkey on Thanksgiving?)

2 rolls of butcher paper—one to cover work space, one to become wrapping paper

Assorted holiday stamps

Assorted holiday stencils

Three 4-ounce bottles of red craft paint

Three 4-ounce bottles of green craft paint

Three 4-ounce bottles of white craft paint

Three 4-ounce bottles of gold craft paint.

Assorted paintbrushes, at least 1 per guest

1 disposable sponge paintbrush per guest

Blank note cards–quantity to be determined by the number of holiday greeting cards to be sent by each guest

1 yardstick

30 gold paper or plastic plates

20 gold paper napkins

10 sets of cutlery

10 cocktail glasses

---

tional, fun, and *sisterhood*-building activities for these meetings. Your *rush group* is very exclusive, and should consist of no more than ten lucky *rushees*. Your *chapter development* will consist of a cookie swap, holiday card making project, and wrapping paper project.

Decorations? It's called your Christmas tree, and we're hoping it's artificial. You put it up after you ate the turkey, and you can even leave it up until after your last New Martini's Eve guest leaves. A live tree is really nothing more than a fire hazard and a cleaning nightmare. If you're still hung up on pine scent, buy some potpourri.

Other than that, your decor is defined by the crafting. So set down butcher paper on your work spaces. If you don't have a craft room, the dining room table and a large coffee table work just fine. Ideally there should be three distinct party spaces: an area in your kitchen for cookie tasting and swapping, a large table for gift-wrap making, and a smaller table for card stamping.

Why are the plates gold? Well, just because you're working doesn't mean you aren't a princess!

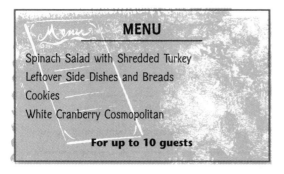

MENU

Spinach Salad with Shredded Turkey

Leftover Side Dishes and Breads

Cookies

White Cranberry Cosmopolitan

For up to 10 guests

Spinach Salad with Shredded Turkey

Studies have shown that the average American gains 7 pounds during the holiday season. The last thing we ever want an RSG member to be is average. Fight against mediocrity with salad.

Shredded leftover turkey

Three 6-ounce bags of precut, prewashed spinach salad with dried cranberries and almonds (If dried cranberries and almonds must be purchased separately, buy 3 ounces each, to be mixed as 1 ounce per item, per bag)

1 bottle low-sugar, fat-free balsamic vinaigrette

The prep for this main course begins at Thanksgiving cleanup. You have to deal with that uneaten turkey somehow. Section it off on the bone and place it in a sealable container. Leaving the meat on the bone will prevent the meat from drying out.

The morning of your party, remove the white meat sections and shred them with a fork and knife. Open the bags of spinach salad and place in a large, pretty serving bowl. Toss in the dried cranberries, the almonds, and the shredded turkey. Offer your guests a low-sugar, fat-free balsamic vinaigrette dressing. Who knew leftovers and bagged salad could be this elegant?

Leftover Side Dishes and Bread

Once again, we must grant you creative liberty. Problem is, we don't know what you served and what's left over. We do recommend foisting your fattiest leftovers on your guests. The more you get rid of, the less you'll have around to eat. Set out an array with some serving pieces.

Cookies

One of the many purposes of this party is to ease your baking stress and expose your household to new holiday traditions and tastes. For that reason, each guest will be asked to bring four dozen cookies from their favorite recipe. Why four dozen? One per guest to sample at the party and roughly 30 cookies for each guest to pass off as their own creations at home, work, or whenever cookies are required throughout the holiday season.[1]

White Cranberry Cosmopolitan

Nothing says holiday like the flavor of cranberries and nothing feels more decadent than slowly sipping a cosmo while spending the afternoon with your girlfriends. However, in the interest of protecting your projects from any and all "party foul" spillage, we opt for the white cranberry cosmopolitan here. Few television shows have portrayed the concepts of *sisterhood* and *chapter development* as profoundly as *Sex and the City* did. So in honor of Carrie, Samantha, Charlotte, and Miranda, the signature cocktail for this *chapter development* is the cosmopolitan. Besides, there isn't much else that goes with leftover turkey. While cosmos are normally a lovely shade of pink, you're probably using a lot of red paint at this party, and the drinks should never clash if you can help it. So, it's important to use white cranberry juice.

Two 64-ounce bottles white cranberry juice
3 liters vodka (the most expensive brand you can afford)
¾ cup lime juice

In a cocktail shaker with ice, combine 3 ounces of the white cranberry juice, 2½ ounces of the vodka, and a splash of lime juice. Shake, strain, and serve the cosmo in a classy martini glass. After the second one you'll be explaining how you want Santa to bring you a pair of Manolos.

While we normally advocate serving the signature cocktail punch-bowl style, making the cosmos one at a time won't be a huge hassle for a more intimate gathering. Plus New Martini's Eve is just around the corner, so your girlfriends may need inspiration for their upcoming entry. If you need to, borrow an extra shaker, put the recipe on the counter, and tell the women to help themselves.

---

1. The Society of Recovering Sorority Girls would never urge a woman to sample each of the ten cookies in a single sitting, but the rules of good hostessing require you to demonstrate equal love for each guests' offering.

MAKE THE MOOD COME ALIVE

Chapter development is light on mood as the focus is on the activity. However, we would never suggest that you proceed down this path without making sure Christmas music is playing in the background. Or if you happen to have some old Claymation holiday specials on DVD, show them. They may be a little distracting, but nostalgia is good, especially during the holidays and with your close girlfriends.

Now let's discuss the division of labor. Each guest is instructed in the invitation to bring four dozen cookies, the quantity of blank note cards needed for her Christmas card list, and any holiday stencils, stamps, paints, etc. We've already explained how the cookie part works, let's talk about Christmas cards.

Remember how you made those lovely handwritten invitations for *Beaujolais Nouveau Est Arrivé*? Making Christmas cards is quite similar. Use stencils or stamps to come up with a custom-made holiday greeting. But where does the paint go? Smart girl, you bought extra paper or plastic plates to use as individual palettes. Because everyone sends those Christmas "letters" these days, you really don't need to worry about writing any message inside other than a simple Merry Christmas or Happy Holi-

days. Boom! Your Christmas cards are done. You'll actually want to start addressing them as you sit there gabbing with your girlfriends, sipping cosmos and nibbling on cookies.

Making wrapping paper is very similar. Using a yardstick, section out the second roll of butcher paper into one-, two-, and three-foot sections. If you have craft scissors with decorative edges, use them to cut the paper. Next, use the stencils or stamps to add color and interest to this designer gift packaging. If you're really a perfectionist and this is not enough description for you, they write whole books about making cards and wrapping paper. Buy one. You can even set them out for your guests to review for ideas. They may be your friends, but they can't all be as clever as you are.

TAKING YOUR PARTY FROM GREAT TO FIRST RATE (OR HOW WE DID IT)

Have your guests bring copies of their recipes. You can assemble the recipes into a decorative cookbook and later present that item to your guests as part of their Christmas gift from you.

If your guests are all close friends, instead of buying gifts for each one, have a gift-swap name drawing. This saves you time and allows you to receive one small Coach bag instead of five-scented-candle sets. Under no circumstances are guests to receive gifts via a Yankee Gift Swap.[2]

Other activities for your guests may include wrapping already purchased holiday presents. Your home is a safe haven for carefully selected trinkets that you are trying to hide from the prying eyes of their recipients. This is especially handy for people with Santa Claus–aged children.

Remember, as we've told you from the beginning, focus on a few key elements and the fun will come. No sense in trying to do too much and ending up more overwhelmed than a kid with ADD at the amusement park.

 **TIMELINE**

Start telling your girlfriends about the party the first week of November and determine who will be in town over Thanksgiving weekend. Next, encourage friends who are able to attend to begin to procure supplies, assemble their card lists, and buy presents early. Send e-mail invitations with this information as well as instructions to bring 4 dozen cookies to swap. This first e-mail is sent shortly after you find out who will be in town to attend.

Third week of November—Send e-mail reminders to your guests, inventory your craft supplies. Whatever is still needed can be procured on your Thanksgiving dinner shopping trip. After all, the craft store is always right next to the grocery.

The night before the party—Bake your cookies.[3]

The morning of the party—Start your holiday workout regimen. Straighten the house.

45 minutes before the party—Cover the work spaces with butcher paper. Shred the turkey and remove the spinach salad from the bags, toss in dried cranberries, almonds, and

---

2. In their December 2003 press release, the Society of Recovering Sorority Girls declared war on the Yankee Gift Swap. Thus, it would be poor form for a *rushee* to host one. For those of you unfamiliar with the horror of the Yankee Gift Swap, a hostess directs her guests to bring a gift of low monetary value (aka crap) to a gathering. All of the gifts are placed in a bag or pile and the guests draw numbers. Guests pick and unwrap their gift in ascending numerical order. Once all the gifts have been distributed, the guest who selected last gets to jettison her gift and take one opened by another guest. Thus all the gifts can be redistributed in descending numerical order.

3. There is no preparation beauty ritual for *chapter development*. We assume you got pretty for Thanksgiving and a manicure would not hold up against the crafting and baking.

the turkey. Mix the first shaker of cosmos. Heat Thanksgiving leftovers to serve as sidedishes.

A WORD ABOUT . . .
SISTERHOOD

Sisterhood. Sigh. It makes your faithful founders all teary-eyed. But for the uninitiated, we'll offer an explanation. *Sisterhood* is a term used to describe the close companionship of a group of women. This means being able to turn to one another for emotional, and in some cases physical, support at all times. It's having girlfriends who will celebrate everything from your new job to your new hairstyle with you. When a silly boy breaks your heart, they move into action, proffering Ben and Jerry's ice cream, white wine, and several rounds of "Well, we always thought you were too good for him." These women are your sounding board. They won't agree with you every single time, but they are always guaranteed to give you an honest opinion.

Some may think *sisterhood* is as outdated as the suffrage movement, but we disagree. The need for *sisterhood* is as great today as it was in the mid- to late-nineteenth century when sororities were just getting started. The women who founded the first sororities were teenagers, often away from home for the first time. While we may be a little older and facing different challenges, the need for encouragement remains the same. Having women who will point out the irony life presents will make your journey toward personal success as important as the goal. A close-knit circle of friends creates a new type of family, providing structure and comfort while giving you plenty of room to develop and define yourself.

So how is a *sisterhood* created? Through shared experiences, activities, and laughter. Just give it time. Soon you'll find your modern-day *sisterhood*, whether it's preparing to face the holidays, celebrating someone's success, or formulating revenge for some guy stupid enough to try to break your heart.

ARE YOU READY TO ACCEPT YOUR BID TO PLEDGE THE SOCIETY OF RECOVERING SORORITY GIRLS?

Please circle the correct answer.

1. It's December 15. Have the invitations for your New Martini's Eve Party gone out yet?

Yes   No

2. Have you ever spent three hours scouring the Internet for the perfect tequila cocktail to accent your party?

Yes   No

3. Have you ever gone to a specific restaurant or bar for the express purpose of tasting their signature dish or drink and referred to it as "party research"?

Yes   No

4. Have you ever refused an invitation to a friend's party because you knew their failure to properly articulate the party's theme would annoy you?

Yes   No

5. Have you mastered appropriate RSVP technique?

Yes   No

6. Have you ever bought a kitchen appliance simply because you needed it to prepare a signature dish for one of your parties?

Yes   No

7. Have you ever invited people you don't like into your home simply because you knew they would round out your guest list?

Yes   No

8. Do you own a fog machine, a galvanized steel tub, or a crystal punch bowl?

Yes   No

9. In the last 4 weeks, has someone asked you when your next party will be?

Yes   No

10. At least three times in the past year, have you found yourself covered in paint used for a decoration, an invitation or a party favor?

Yes   No

11. Are the police threatening to arrest you if another neighbor complains about those loud parties or all the illegal parking they cause?

Yes   No

12. Have you ever invented a holiday just to have people over?

Yes   No

If you answered yes to **0–2** of the above questions, you should wait at least a semester before *pledging* Rho Sigma Gamma. In the meantime read this book again and regularly consult the official RSG Web site, www.recoveringsororitygirls.com. You are doing something wrong, or just not having enough parties! In the alternative, you may need to seek therapy or at least spend some serious self-reflection on Brooksie's rant "Don't Be Beige." A licensed, clinical therapist can walk you through it.

If you answered yes to **3–6** of the above questions, you are ready to accept your *bid*, but you may have a tough time making it through your *pledge period* if you keep hanging out with your current friends. We think they're holding you back. Your *Big Sister* will help you overcome this challenge.

If you answered yes to **7–11** of the above questions, you're bucking to be the *pledge class* president. Go out and buy yourself *letters* and a tiara. Your friends might think it's weird at first. After all, you'll be adjusting to a new way of life while sporting your lovely, jeweled headpiece, and they won't. But it's O.K. Not everyone is as party savvy as you are, and you should take pride in your party accomplishments.

If you answered yes to **all 12** questions, we're calling the police. Clearly you've been stalking either Morgan or Brooksie!

EXTRA CREDIT
Your friends already call you their party goddess.

Yes   No

You're already a Rho Sigma Gamma! Put your official party tiara on and don't take it off. Keep planning those parties, and never hesitate to invite Morgan and Brooksie to your next fete.

Chapter Ten

DECEMBER

BLACK TIE
AND TIARA
INFORMAL FORMAL

Because you're now an official RSG Pledge, let's celebrate in style!

CONCEPT

Sadly, everyday life does not provide ample opportunity to wear velvet, satin, silk, or tiaras. For this reason, the indomitable spirit of RSG dictates that at least once a year, you create an opportunity for such wardrobing.

Many women in college join sororities for an opportunity to wear pretty dresses and dance with boys. Something would be wrong if Rho Sigma Gamma didn't give its members the same privilege. Herein is your opportunity to do so. Seize it, and do not look back. You are now a full-fledged *pledge* of Rho Sigma Gamma. Understanding this philosophy will be crucial to your ability to complete your *pledge* period and become a *sister*.

Let's talk about what makes a party semi-formal. Well, you put it on the invitation. This lets people know the most important detail— what to wear and what *not* to wear. But you also have to ratchet up the level of sophistication and style in your decorations, menu, and mood. So let's get started, *pledges*.

DECORATIONS

A well-lit and decorated Christmas tree—
   extra points for matching ornaments
1 keg of platinum (an RSG color) curling
   ribbon
3 strands of 100 white Christmas tree lights
   per 1,500 square feet of party space
20 tea lights
4 potted poinsettias
1 small disco ball
Linens for your food table—white or holiday,
   both acceptable
30 paper or plastic red or green plates
40 red or green paper napkins
30 sets of cutlery
40 champagne flutes or small plastic tum-
   bler-size glasses

It's December. We haven't forgotten you still have obligations in addition to *pledging*. But your Christmas tree is already up, and your home is decorated. Good, RSG *pledge*, you're nearly finished! Fasten those additional strands of white Christmas tree lights throughout your party space at eye level, then scatter and light the tea lights.

Have you forgotten everything *rush* taught you? There is no party that cannot be improved by the addition of curling ribbon. You know the drill. Give it the treatment: chandeliers, stemware, and anywhere you would want confetti, but don't want the mess. Set the poinsettias in prominent places, such as by the entryway and as a centerpiece on your food table. No, it's not necessarily a lot. But like an RSG *pledge class*, style cannot be measured in quantity. It's all about quality. Think about that when you wonder why you accepted your *bid*.

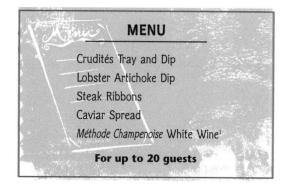

MENU

Crudités Tray and Dip
Lobster Artichoke Dip
Steak Ribbons
Caviar Spread
Méthode Champenoise White Wine[1]

For up to 20 guests

---

1. As we have previously stated, the Society of Recovering Sorority Girls strongly encourages its members to drink American; therefore, champagne method wine is strongly preferred to Champagne. Just say no to the tyranny of the French nomenclature system unless you are celebrating Beaujolais nouveau.

Crudité Tray and Dip

The holiday's colors are red, white, and green. Therefore, your vegetables must follow suit. You are using green and red bell peppers, asparagus spears, cherry tomatoes, and broccoli florets. Yum! The dip is the white element.

Two 8-ounce bags precut raw broccoli florets

**2 red bell peppers, seeded and sliced
    lengthwise into narrow wedges**

**2 green bell peppers, seeded and sliced
    lengthwise into narrow wedges**

Two 8-ounce containers cherry tomatoes

1 pound fresh asparagus spears

Two 8-ounce containers fat-free ranch dip

Lobster Artichoke Dip

**Two 8-ounce packages Lobster Delights or 1
    pound fresh lobster tails**

One 8-ounce can quartered artichoke hearts

One 8-ounce package reduced-fat cream cheese

**1 cup shredded cheese (Parmesan, Asiago, and
    Romano–blend works best)**

1 cup fat-free mayonnaise

1 teaspoon fresh chopped garlic

1 tablespoon vodka

1 tablespoon powdered mustard

1 tablespoon paprika

2 loaves of French bread, thinly sliced

Preheat the oven to 350 degrees. Dump the following ingredients into the bowl of your electric mixer: both packages of the lobster, the quartered artichoke hearts, reduced-fat cream cheese, shredded cheese, fat-free mayonnaise, chopped garlic, one tablespoon of vodka, and mustard. Mix for 2 minutes; scrape down the sides of the mixing bowl and mix for another minute. Pour the mixture into a three-quart casserole dish. Sprinkle the paprika on top. Bake for 25 minutes, until lightly browned and bubbling. Serve with the thinly sliced French bread. This dish is "Jackie O" elegant. Pretend like it was hard when someone compliments you on it.

Steak Ribbons

You will need about forty 6-inch wood skewers for this dish.

3.5 pounds lean, boneless rib-eye steak

One 10-ounce bottle Worcestershire sauce

One 3.12-ounce can steak seasoning

Trim the fat from the steak and discard. Slice the steak into thin strips, approximately ½ inch wide. Thread one strip of steak onto a wood skewer, alternating from side to side to create a ribbon look. You will need to thread close to the tip of the skewer but once you have finished creating the ribbon slide the steak strip down to the center. Place the steak ribbon skewers in an ovenproof glass baking dish. Once you have filled the bottom of the dish with the steak skewers, liberally coat them with Worcestershire sauce and steak seasoning. Add a second layer of steak skewers and repeat the Worcestershire and seasoning. Depending on the size of your baking dish, you may need to repeat this process using a second dish or a casserole. Layering more than two sets of steak ribbons will cause them to cook unevenly. Cover the dish with foil or wrap and let the steak ribbons marinate overnight in the refrigerator. Preheat the oven to 400 degrees. Bake for 12 minutes. This should yield approximately 40 steak ribbon skewers.

Caviar Spread

Caviar, once a luxury known only to kings and the wealthy in Russia and Iran, is now widely available both online and in the average Middle-America grocery store. Nevertheless, caviar retains its luxurious cachet, and you are all about cachet. You already have steak and lobster; you might as well complete the set.

The thing about caviar is that it is very salty and not necessarily an attractive food to eat. A little, therefore, goes a long way and at these prices, thank goodness for that!

1 small jar red caviar, 2 ounces
1 small jar black caviar, 2 ounces
60 unsalted, light crackers
Two 8-ounce round containers fat-free or low-fat
**   whipped cream cheese**

Keep in mind simple preparation is the best. We recommend presenting your red caviar and black caviar in separate small silver bowls, on ice, and on separate trays. Provide a small dessert spoon for each and place unsalted light crackers around each bowl. To one side of each of your caviar and cracker trays, on a salad-sized china plate, empty one tub of the fat-free or low-fat whipped cream cheese. Cut the cream cheese out of the tub if necessary to maintain the rounded, cake-like mold. Place a sprinkling of caviar in the center and insert a decorative spreader into each. Watch friends stare at you in admiration.

Méthode Champenoise White Wine

2 cases *méthode Champenoise* white wine

Surf, turf, and caviar. Now, the final luxury, sparkling white wines (aka *Méthode Champenoise* White Wine). Chill the wine and then pour into the appropriate stemware. Many people find opening champagne intimidating. As an RSG *rushee*, it doesn't have to be that way for you.

It wouldn't be a sorority if members didn't get some benefits out of membership. Girls join sororities for friendship and parties, but also for resources. We can't offer you the university exam file, but RSG can offer you something better, at least for your adult life: Morgan's sure-fire champagne-opening method.

As you know, the Society of Recovering Sorority Girls opposes, on moral grounds, any activity leading to the waste of alcohol. One of the most insidious forms of alcohol waste is improper champagne uncorking technique. Any method that involves shaking, spraying, spillage, or lack of cork control, while glorified in film and in the media, is frankly wrong.

Step 1: Appropriately chill your champagne.

Step 2: Take the bottle of champagne and place it on a hard, stable surface like a table or counter.

Step 3: Remove the foil and metal cork restraint.

Step 4: Holding the bottle steady with one hand, take your dominant hand and place it over the top of the bottle and cork in a protective manner. Slowly twist upward on the cork, easing it gently from the mouth of the bottle. You will hear a pop, but lose no wine! Also, as you have maintained control of the cork, your windows, glassware, and your guests' eyes will still be intact.

Step 5: Enjoy and *salut!*

MAKE THE MOOD COME ALIVE

This is your first Black Tie and Tiara Informal Formal! Aren't you excited? Good, because you will need to package that excitement into the mood of this party. Excitement ingredient number one is the semiformal attire. The preparty buzz should be "What are you wearing?" Remember how pretty and special you felt the first time you wore an official homecoming or prom dress? That's how your female guests should all feel. What about the guys you ask? If the females are dressed to the nines, the boys will be on their best behavior and flirting to impress.

Excitement ingredient number two is a dance floor. It doesn't have to be huge, but you will need to designate a certain portion of your party space for this purpose. Push all the furniture up against the walls if you need to make more room. If you have an unfinished basement, you are the luckiest girl in the world—you have an instant dance floor that just screams rave party. On the decoration list for this party, we told you to get a small disco ball, but we waited to explain why. We recognize that if used incorrectly or with a different party, a disco ball would be downright tacky. But here, it fits your theme and clearly designates a defined space as the dance floor. So hang it up over this predesignated area.

Now you're all dressed up, standing on a dance floor. We need to talk about music. Start the party off with some classic instrumental holiday tunes. As you hear the bottles of champagne uncorking, start to transition the music to more danceable songs. There are all kinds of dance party music compilation CDs on the market. Just be sure the third or fourth song is one you really love. For Brooksie, nothing beats "Bizarre Love Triangle" by New Order or B-52's "Love Shack." For Morgan it's Blink-182's "Dammit" or Beyoncé's "Crazy in Love." Proudly proclaim, "I love this song, let's dance!" Then grab the nearest or cutest boy who has had at least two glasses of champagne and begin dancing. Others will join you.

TAKE YOUR PARTY FROM GREAT TO FIRST RATE (OR HOW WE DID IT)

Add a simple, but decadent-sounding dessert to the menu. Christmas petit-fours, preferably made with white chocolate, are a perfect addition.

Make the memories of your first Black Tie and Tiara Informal Formal last forever with party pictures. Typically, sororities hire professional photographers to take pictures at their social events. Add that touch by scattering a few disposable cameras throughout the party space and encourage your guests to take lots of pictures.

Every formal dance offers a party favor. How else do you get the guys to agree to go? You don't have to go all out and order T-shirts, but you can make cheap picture frames. Just purchase the needed quantity of clear plastic frames at the craft store. Don't spend more than a dollar per frame. Then use stickers and a paint pen to personalize the frame. Write "Black Tie and Tiara Informal Formal" and the date on the frame with the paint pen. Add stickers of champagne bottles, flutes, or black ties in the corners. Once you have bought the supplies, you can accomplish the personalization of your party favors while watching one episode of your current fave TV show.

Basically if you've gone to all the trouble of putting on a semiformal dress, you might as well take the party from great to first rate. There's really no other way to do it.

 TIMELINE

Clearly, this is a new dress occasion. Be kind to your girlfriends and let them know about your intentions to host this party prior to the all-day dining feast we call Thanksgiving. Besides, the day after Thanksgiving is the perfect opportunity to find *the* dress. The official e-mail invitation needs to go out early too. The party gods are most ruthless between Thanksgiving and New Year's. Don't let your party be the one guests regret due to other social events.

Thanksgiving Day—Put up your Christmas tree and holiday decorations.

Two weeks before the party—Inventory your decorations. Buy any items you need. Purchase your dress, as well as any accessories you might need. If you don't already own a tiara, you have to get one immediately. Start wearing it and practice your tiara attitude.

One week before the party—Decide on your music plan. Procure the music.

The day before the party—Tidy your party space. Hang the white Christmas tree lights.

Arrange the tea lights. Create your dance floor. Basically get the decorating done and out of the way. Go to the grocery. Marinate the steak ribbons.

The morning of the party—Blend the ingredients needed to make the Lobster Artichoke Dip, but do not bake it yet. Just put it in the fridge for now. Next, give your party space the curling ribbon treatment. You have the remainder of the day to primp. Make us proud!

An hour before the party—Prepare the Crudités Tray and Dip. Slice the French bread. Arrange the food table.

Forty-five minutes before the party—Bake the Lobster Artichoke Dip.

Fifteen minutes before the party—Remove the Lobster Artichoke Dip from the oven. Arrange your caviar, crackers, and spread. Bake the steak ribbons. Now that the cooking is done, put on that informal formal dress.

Ten minutes before the party—Uncork the first bottle of champagne. Toast yourself congratulations on becoming a Rho Sigma Gamma *pledge*.

Five minutes before the party—Light the tea lights. Make sure all the Christmas tree lights are plugged in.

A WORD ABOUT . . . SEMIFORMAL ATTIRE

What is semiformal attire? It's fancier than cocktail party attire but does not rise to the level of black tie. It is the rare air between the two. Technically, you may be wearing a cocktail gown, but you will have added shoes, purse, and jewelry to take it to the next level or from great to first rate, if you will.

Semiformal attire should make you feel sexy, as if you are the star of your own show. Note—semiformal attire excludes any brides-maid's dresses, no matter how much you paid or how often some bride claimed you could wear it again for a special occasion. You are not a backup singer here!

So what fits this definition? Those fabrics that everyday life presents very few opportunities to wear. Silk, satin, and velvet or the "celebration" fabrics all fit the description. But fabric alone does not semiformal attire make. A neckline not suited for the office and the occasional hint of beadwork meet part two of the semiformal definition. But don't forget to complete the look with a pair of strappy shoes that are completely impractical, the most expensive jewelry you own, and a handbag too small for functionality.

In short, life—especially an RSG life—is to be celebrated. Celebrate by looking your best and by using your home-entertaining efforts to create opportunities for you and your friends to live a life less ordinary.

Now that you've *rushed* Rho Sigma Gamma and accepted your *bid*, it's time to learn our creed and prepare yourself for the party challenges of *sisterhood*.

THE CREED OF THE SOCIETY OF RECOVERING SORORITY GIRLS

We believe that when properly planned, executed, and hosted, a party is a social service.

We believe in the power of theme.

We believe activities are needed to spark conversations among soon-to-be friends.

We believe parties are to be enjoyed; home entertaining isn't a job; it's a low-stress adventure designed to explore your creativity and invigorate your social tribe.

We believe the collegiate Greek experience offers friendship, support, and valuable life skills.

We believe that those skills can be adopted by women everywhere regardless of the existence or absence of collegiate Greek affiliation.

Because, above all, we believe it is never too late or too early for any woman to realize the *sisterhood* that is the Society of Recovering Sorority Girls.

We are Rho Sigma Gamma. A way to entertain. A way to party. A way to live.

GLOSSARY OF SORORITY SPEAK TERMS

Bid—An invitation to pledge a sorority.

Big Sister—An older sister assigned to help transition a *pledge,* referred to as her *little sister,* into the sisterhood.

Brothers—Fraternity boys.

Bump—An introduction a hostess makes between two guests, providing them with a topic of conversation.

Chapter(s)—A word often used to identify a single, local unit of a larger national sorority.

Chapter Development—A meeting of an individual unit (chapter) during which *sisters* and *pledges* participate in educational, fun, and sisterhood-building activities.

Collegiate(s)—Sorority girls still in college.

Letters—Refers to articles of clothing which bear the Greek insignia of a sorority.

Mixer—A social event where a group of women meets a group of men for a short period of time that is primarily consumed by a game or activity.

National Executive Office—Rho Sigma Gamma's headquarters.

Panhellenic—The governing body of national sororities. It seeks to foster an overall pro-Greek and prosorority attitude among the different national sororities.

Pledge—A woman participating in a sorority's new member education program, but not yet initiated into the secret ritual of the sorority. She refers to her fellow *pledges* as her *pledge sisters* and together they compose the *pledge class.* *Pledge* can also be used as a verb to describe assimilating into the sorority.

Risk Management—A policy designed to enforce local, state, and federal alcohol consumption laws, and preserve the chapter's general liability insurance.

Rotation—The flow of a party. The act of circulating throughout the room, talking to all of your guests.

Rush—The mutual selection recruitment proceeding used by Greek organizations. Women going through the process are referred to as *rushees.* The first step is composed of open parties, attended by all *rushees*; this is followed by various invitation-only parties, which means that *rushees* must be invited back. The final round is a preference party, to which only the most desired *rushees* receive an invitation.

Rush Group—The group of individuals invited to your event.

Sister—An active, initiated member of a sorority.

Sisterhood—A group of women who share a strong friendship.

Social Chair—The sister responsible for planning social events and leader of the *Social Committee.*

INDEX OF RECIPES

ABOUT THE AUTHORS

Kristina "Morgan" Rose is a second-generation sorority girl, having pledged Phi Mu her sophomore year of college. Morgan is a graduate of American University and the Catholic University of America Columbus School of Law. After spending 4 years in the Tampa, Florida, area practicing corporate law, Morgan and her husband, Joe Rose, relocated to Anne Arundel County, Maryland, where she continues to pursue the perfect party, the perfect recipe, and the perfect cocktail while also continuing to practice law.

Deandra "Brooskie" Brooks participated in sorority rush, accepting Phi Mu's bid during her first month at American University. After graduation she began a career in politics and has applied her sorority-girl organizational skills to the Heritage Foundation, the California State Legislature, the U.S. Congress, and the Federal Aviation Administration. When she's not trying to keep the "party" in her political party, Brooksie is typically busy planning her next big social event.

Both Morgan and Brooksie agree that their greatest accomplishment has been founding the Society of Recovering Sorority Girls, aka Rho Sigma Gamma. They look forward to seeing all of their readers and Rho Sigma Gamma members in the virtual sorority house at www.recovering-sororitygirls.com and at the next Rho Sigma Gamma event.